TREKKER GIRL

Life a
How I Learned to Live and Love Life as a
Thrombosis Survivor

Dawne Elizabeth Archer

This book is dedicated to thrombosis survivors.
I am lucky enough to be one; my dad wasn't.

*****

This work would never have seen the light of day
without the constant guidance and encouragement of
E Van Johnson: mentor and patient editor.

Plus, the support of friends and family who were
guinea pigs from my first garbled scribblings to where
we are now.

Sarah, Fred and Hector: my second family. I am so
lucky you are in my life.

Bernie: friend and co-conspirator in all our adventures,
your support and love is immeasurable.

Thank you

*****

*EVERY SIX SECONDS A PERSON DIES
FROM VTE GLOBALLY*

*THROMBOSIS (throm-bo'sis) the formation or
presence of a thrombus*

*THROMBUS (throm'bus) a solid mass formed in the
vessels from constituents of blood*

*VENOUS THROMBOEMBOLISM formation of clot in
a vein eg., Deep Vein Thrombosis in the leg, part of
which can break off and travel to the lung forming a
Pulmonary Embolism*

*VTE as opposed to Arterial clots such as Heart Attacks
or Strokes*

*Taken from the Thrombosis UK website www.thrombosisuk.org and reproduced
with their kind permission*

Contents

INTRODUCTION

First things first: thank you for buying this book. I will be donating all the profits directly to Thrombosis UK (charity number 1090540) to help this amazing organisation in their work in education, research and support in the field of thrombosis.

They achieve remarkable things with very little; most of the people directly involved are volunteers, keeping costs down. Both health professionals and the general public can learn to "Spot the Clots", a campaign full of information that may save your life or that of someone close to you.

We all need to be aware of the tell-tale signs of a Deep Vein Thrombosis. These can range from swelling and tenderness in the leg to discolouration and pain. However, 80% of DVTs show no symptoms and that is why they can be hard to diagnose.

Pulmonary Embolisms usually bring on shortness of breath and chest pain, and a sufferer may collapse. These are symptoms, obvious and hard to ignore, although sometimes still confused with other issues.

The Thrombosis UK website is a brilliant resource so check it out at www.thrombosisuk.org

This organisation started as Lifeblood: The Thrombosis Charity back in 2002. Since I did the trek, they have become known as Thrombosis UK. Photos of me will show a Lifeblood t-shirt but I have chosen to refer to them under their current name.

Secondly, thrombosis is a complex subject. The information and opinions in this book are based on my limited knowledge and experience. Please do not rely on anything I have said relating to medical matters as it may not be relevant to you and medical opinion moves forward rapidly.

I am learning more every day, and, in the light of updated information, I have changed some things I used to do as a matter of course. For example, flight socks which fit badly can be potentially harmful, restricting circulation. I don't wear them anymore. However, if they are prescribed for you and properly fitted, or you find them comfortable and easy to wear, then don't stop. Everyone's situation is different, so please follow the advice you are given that is directly applicable to you.

If you have never come across any clotting disorders before, Factor V Leiden is pronounced as Factor Five Leiden but is usually written using the Roman numeral for five.

Having a blood clot is traumatic. For some people, the whole thing can be short-lived. Perhaps a DVT that may result in three or six months of anticoagulant treatment and nothing further. Yet, there is the risk of reoccurrence, and it is always there, in the back of your mind. Every ache and pain is assessed in the light of your experience.

A Pulmonary Embolism is always a shock with potentially life-threatening consequences. My brush with death changed my life forever.

It is an issue many of us struggle with. Not only survivor guilt (why did I get through it and my dad didn't) but a complete reassessment of your life and what to do next.

Lifetime anticoagulation treatment is not something I currently have to face, but it is a "game changer", and you have to learn to live with a "new normal".

ADDITION: Since 2018, the prospect of lifetime anticoagulation treatment has become my "new normal".

I did struggle with this issue, but it is potentially saving my life, and little has changed for me, other than taking care over physical challenges.

Life-changing it may be, but I hope this book will allow you to see that the risks can be managed, and life lived to its fullest, despite the diagnosis of a clotting disorder. We can't live our lives in fear. I took control by affecting those things I can (like diet, weight, fitness etc.), which is my way of dealing with it.

This trek wasn't as much fun as it should have been. I struggled to achieve my goal; you'll have to read on to find out why.

I spent much of the time in a bubble of my own making, not sharing my experience as much as I may otherwise have done. So, my fellow trekkers are bit players in my drama, sketchily portrayed, and for that I can only apologise. They were a great bunch of people, all raising money for causes close to their hearts.

The same goes for my recollections; any inaccuracies or omissions are down to me.

Van Johnson is my writing mentor. His guidance and input have been invaluable, and I would not have produced this book without his constant support. I can only thank him for his endless reserves of patience, especially with the interminable editing. Van's historical fiction books can be found on Amazon under E Van Johnson.

Sarah, my companion in this adventure, was then and still is a star. I feel lucky to know her and her entire family.

Bernie, my "partner in crime" and usual travelling companion, is the only person who can put up with me on a daily basis. Thanks - for everything.

CHAPTER ONE
Family Trauma

I asked myself, not for the first time, 'What was I doing?' How had I ended up in the Sahara Desert, slumped wearily in a dusty camping chair?

Collapsed right alongside me, Sarah, my childhood friend and plucky travelling companion, looked every one of her fifty-two years. Goodness knows I wasn't any better; our bodies were feeling the pressure.

I hadn't expected this: boots held together with gaffer tape, painkillers at the ready and every move a triumph of determination.

Soaked in sweat, with sand stuck to the layers of high strength suntan lotion, I felt unbearably itchy and very smelly.

I had been determinedly using two walking poles to push myself through the ever-shifting sands, taking great care not to jar my already ravaged back.

Having suffered potentially fatal blood clots at a relatively young age, I was trekking to raise funds for the charity Thrombosis UK. Anyone who has survived them will realise I already had enough to deal with.

Losing my precious sun hat was the straw that broke the camel's back. It was no joke. It was essential protection against the murderous power of the sun. The intense Sahara heat, dehydration and prolonged activity were a dangerous and possibly deadly combination for me. With my fair skin and despite thick hanks of blonde hair, it left me unprotected against the harsh and unforgiving elements.

How had I got myself into this predicament?

Thirty years ago, the pain, sharp and fierce in my chest, woke me up with a start. As I fought to think straight, I had no notion of how this moment was about to change my life forever.

I had suffered a Deep Vein Thrombosis and a Pulmonary Embolism (blood clots in my leg and lung). Still today, my heart races as the memories come flooding back; I feel a cold sweat creeping across my body as I remember the intense pain sharpening with each breath I took.

I now realise how close I came to death; a shocking realisation at any age but particularly at a relatively young twenty-six.

DVT is often thought of as related to long flights and periods of inactivity. It may be obvious from swelling, redness and pain in the leg. However, they often show no symptoms at all. These blood clots can, and do, kill.

A piece of mine had broken off and travelled into my lung causing the sharp and shockingly debilitating pain in the back of my chest.

The first visit to my local doctor turned out to be pointless. She took blood tests, but there was no action to investigate or alleviate my suffering. She seemed to underestimate the agony I felt. It was hard for me to describe and proved impossible for her to locate.

Each breath I took caused a sharp stab inside my chest as if someone was sticking a knife through my back. It didn't respond to external pressure, and the doctor didn't recognise my symptoms. Sadly, this is often true, even today.

Looking back, I can't believe I suffered in silence but, back then, the doctor's words were sacred, and we would never dare to question them.

Hindsight often enables us to see things more clearly, and I now have so much more knowledge than I had then but, at the time, I began to doubt myself. Was I imagining it or making more of the pain than it really was?

With true "Brit grit", I soldiered on for a week, eating and drinking little, lying on my sofa and rolling off it to get to the toilet. Phone calls with my family elicited no real concern as I kept the truth from them and, probably, from myself. I was in constant and severe discomfort but taking shallow breaths kept things manageable, and the doctor had as good as told me that I was imagining things.

In the end, I couldn't bear it any longer and called my doctor in for a home visit. She dismissed my concerns.

'Well, Dawne, the tests for hepatitis and pneumonia have come back negative. I can't see what the problem is, just get on with things and take aspirin for pain relief if you need it.'

Such was the diagnosis.

Waking up at the end of another week, my chest had started to rattle. I had been lying down for most of a fortnight with no respite from the pain, and this new development frightened me. Moving slowly, I was determined to see another doctor who could reassess my symptoms. The persistent pain and increasing difficulty I had breathing held me in a tight fist of fear.

I was ready for a fight, desperately needing someone to take notice of what I was saying. The pain was intense. How could my doctor dismiss it?

I started to feel very upset and out of my depth, having had to get annoyed and tearful with the dragon of a receptionist to get an appointment. Notoriously protective of their doctors, this lady couldn't see why I wanted to see anyone else. My evident agitation eventually persuaded her that my need was immediate.

As I walked into the consulting room, it was almost as if this new doctor had been expecting me.

'Hello, Dawne. Has there been any change?' It was all I could do to shake my head in despair.

He didn't have many other questions for me. He could see the state I was in, and it was clear that I had been a topic of conversation amongst the doctors there.

'Did you drive here?' he demanded, breaking off from his phone conversation. He then asked the receptionist to call the local hospital.

His abrupt manner was beginning to frighten me. Taking my comments and worries very seriously, he was already making some kind of arrangements. It was all spiralling out of my control.

'Yes,' I replied nervously, wondering why he would ask such a question.

'Drive to the hospital and park in a long-term space. They will be waiting for you in Emergency,' he ordered. There was no kindness or consideration for my feelings, and he was not about to accept any arguments.

I had wanted to be taken seriously, but this was far more than I had expected. My mind was a blank, and I wasn't taking in the urgency in his words. Shocked and upset, I tried to get a grip on my emotions, not knowing what to think.

'But I have to...' I stammered, my mind racing with all the things I thought needed sorting out before I went anywhere near a hospital.

'If you don't go immediately, you will be arriving on a stretcher sooner rather than later, so go straight there. They are expecting you,' he ordered.

Leaving the surgery, I didn't know where to go or what to do. Should I go to the hospital? A persistent voice kept nagging in my head; surely it couldn't be that urgent, or could it? After all, I was still upright and walking, albeit in considerable pain. The doctor had frightened me but was I that ill? It didn't seem real.

We didn't have mobile phones back in the 1980s, so I would have had to go home to ring anyone or find a useable telephone box. There was no one I could call to come and give me some support as none of my family lived nearby.

The stabbing in my chest was growing sharper, increasing as my breath got faster and my heart beat harder.

Having driven slowly and carefully, shaking with fear and anxiety, I managed to find a parking space at the hospital. As I headed towards the doors, I was aware that I had never been there before. Until then, I had been a relatively healthy person, and I was trying to avoid the increasing pain by panting and taking shallow breaths. It wasn't working very well, and I was starting to panic.

'Where's A and E?' I asked another visitor who pointed out the sign above my head; I was standing right underneath it. I hadn't even noticed it from my private bubble of terror.

Following the doctor's orders, I had parked in a long-term space, but the Emergency hospital entrance was at the other side of the building, and I was starting to lose focus. Gasping for air, sweating with the intensely sharp pains piercing my chest, I knew I was in trouble and on the very edge of losing consciousness.

'Where is it? Where is it? God help me!'

'Here! Over here, love,' a nurse shouted, racing towards me with a wheelchair.

'Dawne? It is Dawne, isn't it?' It was all I could do to nod and sink gratefully into the chair.

'Don't worry, love. We've been expecting you. Let's get you into a cubicle. You'll be OK, just try and calm down,' said the welcoming figure in a blue striped dress, holding my hand and speaking gently.

Intensely relieved, I just let go and allowed things to happen, realising help was at hand. I had no idea of the impact my entrance had made. Apparently, I had staggered in through the Emergency doors, on the verge of collapse with sweat blurring my eyesight and fighting for breath as I cast wildly about for assistance.

At this point, I gave in to the fear, pain and exhaustion, oblivious to the intense activity around me and burst into floods of tears.

Brain in a whirl, heart pumping, I still had no idea what to expect. It had been pretty dramatic so far, but what were they going to *do* to me now that I was in the hospital? How long would it take, and most importantly, would it hurt?

I had not yet realised that this was a life-threatening situation.

I was frightened and apprehensive, having so little knowledge of how dangerous blood clots were. Would I need an operation? I don't recall ever thinking I might die, but I do remember the relief that, finally, someone believed that I was not imagining things and that the pain was real.

My doctor had dismissed all the warning signs, and my life was in danger because of her mistaken diagnosis.

Slowly I managed to get my breathing under control again and calmed myself down. Around me, the activity

15

slowed as a nurse came and tried to insert a needle into a vein in my arm, so a drip could be attached.

'Ouch!' I complained, yelping with the unexpected pinch as the needle missed the vein. 'That hurts.'

'OK, Dawne, you need to relax if you can. I'll have to try another one. You have skin like rhino hide,' exclaimed the nurse. Charming. However, I was too distressed to notice the insult.

This time the needle slipped into the back of my hand with no trouble, although I felt much aggrieved about the pain inflicted, a bit like adding insult to injury. It's a silly thing that shouldn't hurt but often does, much to my disgust.

Finally, in bed and flat on my back, I was safely hooked up to a Heparin drip. However, to me at least, no one seemed to be unduly hurried or overly concerned. No one bothered to explain what the contents were at the time, and I was left to rest, although that was impossible with my head spinning, wondering what would happen next and still in agony.

Outside my cubicle, I could hear all sorts of awful noises, and my imagination was running wild. A man was shouting for help because he was bleeding badly from an accident in the garden, a child was screaming, and a woman was complaining about waiting. It was not a restful place to be.

I was left to my own devices for six interminable hours. Apart from the "vampires" who came from Haematology to take blood samples and the occasional nurse who popped in from time to time to check I was still alive, there was no further information offered. I was beginning to wonder if the situation was that serious at all.

Eventually, a nurse appeared.

'Right, Dawne, we need to get these compression stockings on your legs.' Anyone who has ever tried to put these on will know what she meant.

'Toe first aaaaaand … push!' It was a moment of levity in an otherwise horrible day. These tightly fitting, thigh-high elasticated monstrosities are designed to help with blood flow when you are immobile, and, at this point, I had one foot pushing hard against the sturdy nurse as she rolled these infernal things onto each leg. I didn't feel much like laughing, but when she chuckled, I couldn't help but join in at the thought of the ridiculous sight we must have made.

When I was wheeled into a ward full of women recovering from a variety of surgical procedures, I wasn't sure what to make of it all. I settled into bed with my drip attached, still without any proper explanations.

Liking to be in control, I am sure I was a proper pest for the nurses, forever asking questions and querying every treatment.

'What's in this drip? What's the pill for? What's going on? Why does it still hurt when I breathe?'

My frequent questions were met with the same response every time.

'The doctor will be round in the morning and will explain things to you then.'

To me, it was all very unsatisfactory. However, I was in no position to make a fuss. As they say in Devon, I felt "properly sorry for myself", and eventually gave in to the inertia, a thing which is often seen amongst hospital patients; being told what to do and perpetually waiting. I didn't understand what was happening to me or why, and I wasn't happy about it.

Several days later, I was still none the wiser about my situation as they waited for diagnostic tests to confirm their belief that I had clots. I was told the Heparin was a drug to thin my blood but that was about as far as it went.

'No, Dawne, you can't go to the toilet,' the bossy nurse said sharply, reading me the riot act. Of course, I could go, but they weren't about to let me walk down the ward just yet.

'You mustn't put your feet on the floor for the time being,' she explained. So, I had to make do with a bedpan. I was not a "happy bunny".

Bed rest was the order of the day, in complete contrast to today's instructions which are to keep moving.

I was effectively immobilised while the Heparin dripped into a vein to do its job. I have only recently learned that this drug is an anticoagulant and will not disperse a clot that has already formed. What it does do is reduce the ability of the blood to clot and allow the body's natural mechanisms to break them down.

Heparin needs to be given by injection or intravenously to start anticoagulation therapy. Later, it will be reduced whilst an oral version such as Warfarin is introduced and starts to take effect.

Having recovered from the drama of my arrival in A and E, I felt thoroughly fed up as I tried to grasp the full import of what was happening to me. Nurses were sympathetic but no one took the time to allay my fears.

The hospital and its staff, though coldly efficient, gave me no reassurances. I had no real notion of how serious my condition was or how close I had come to losing my life.

As there was no internet then, I had no way of getting information for myself and the doctors just whisked by on their rounds, leaving me feeling small and unimportant.

My family were concerned but unaware of the possible drama lying underneath the surface. They knew very little as communication consisted of an occasional phone call, and I had nothing much to tell them. It would have been a long journey for them to make from Devon to London, and they were waiting to see how things progressed. They would be more helpful to me once I had left the hospital.

With the clarity of hindsight, I can see now that waiting two weeks for a diagnosis had put my life in mortal danger. I had no idea of how it would affect my future and neither did my family. Fortunately, the clot had not lodged in a sector of my lung that would have closed down my air supply and killed me.

I am so lucky to be alive.

I spent the next ten days in the hospital, gradually regaining my equilibrium, trying to make sense of what had happened. An injection of coloured dye through the veins on top of my feet showed a DVT in my leg.

Another procedure involved me breathing into a machine whilst a radioactive tracer injected into my bloodstream showed the embolism in my lung. It was a shock to see it with my own eyes. It sounds horrible, but neither x-ray hurt, and I could see what was happening on a TV screen.

It was a fact. I had two life-threatening blood clots.

I was anxious to get back to my life and itching to get moving and go home. However, I still couldn't understand why breathing was so painful, despite all the treatment. I have since learned that this is normal. Any

19

thrombosis can take a long time to disperse and cause considerable bruising and even permanent damage. It would be many months before I would be pain-free.

'You need to take Warfarin tablets for six months,' the doctor said brusquely.

He was eager to get me discharged so some other needy person could have my bed, but I wasn't about to let him go without asking some questions. I had heard whispers on the ward, hospital gossip.

'Isn't Warfarin rat poison?' I asked, with a tremor in my voice, afraid of the answer I might get.

Avoiding my question, the doctor continued with what he wanted to say, oblivious to my concerns.

'Don't get pregnant,' he added, almost as an afterthought. That put me on the back foot. As a twenty-six-year-old woman, I had most certainly considered having a family. Whilst it wasn't a definite plan, it was quite a shock to be told to forget it for the time being.

'Why not?' I blurted.

'You could bleed to death or have another clot in childbirth. Warfarin can also cause birth defects, and you could bleed to death from an abortion. I don't advise you to risk it. Oh, and you can't take the contraceptive pill.'

What a horrible man. (Ar****le would be more accurate, but I hesitate to offend any sensitive ears – I hope my mum will read this.) I give him no points for bedside manner or empathy with his patient.

That is the memory I have of the stark and uncompromising way in which I was summarily dismissed from the hospital, with instructions to attend a weekly clinic for blood tests to regulate the Warfarin dosage. I left the hospital shell shocked.

Warfarin was, and still is, the standard drug treatment for blood clots; an anticoagulant used to prevent more forming. It is tricky to balance the levels of medication as it interacts with many things, including certain foods, alcohol and other drugs. Side effects can include excessive bleeding, so I had to take care with even the slightest bump or bruise and watch my diet.

Having little understanding of the mechanics or implications of blood clots or this drug, I went wearily home, still in some considerable pain.

****

Fast forward fifteen years to 2001, and I am in a hospital ward with my dad, watching with horror and disbelief the incredible scenes of destruction and death as the World Trade Centre attacks unfolded on the TV screen in front of us.

'What would you do, Dad?' I asked, trying to get a response out of him.

Whilst it was hard to comprehend the tragedy of "jumpers", I hoped to prod him out of his lethargy and get a conversation going again.

Those desperate figures who leapt to their inevitable deaths, faced with a choice of ways to die, will stay with me forever. However, they were the backdrop to my own family trauma.

'Who knows, love. I hope none of us ever have to face such a dilemma.' With that, he drifted off again into a drug-induced sleep.

Watching the drama play out in real time was a distraction from the events of the past three weeks, during which time my dad had gradually deteriorated.

****

Three weeks earlier, on a visit back to Devon, I had planned to spend time with him, catching up on our summer stories. On arrival, he had seemed on good form, so I had driven the short distance to spend a day or two with my mum and her husband.

Twenty-four hours later, I received the phone call that was to change all our lives.

'You need to come back now.' My father was normally a forceful presence, but something in his tone made me jump into the car without delay.

Heading back to his house, I worried about what had changed in such a short space of time. After all, he had seemed fine the day before. As I drove, I thanked my lucky stars that I had not had a glass of wine yet that evening. Being stopped by the Police was all I needed.

My father had called me in something of a panic. When I got to his house, I could see that his ankle had swollen to twice its normal size and his foot was black. He had spent the day in bed, feeling worse as time went on. Calling me was his admission that he needed help.

Dad had been diagnosed with a DVT earlier in the summer and was on the standard six-month regime of Warfarin. He seemed to have things under control, although I wasn't sure how much he was telling me. Living abroad, I had accepted his reassurances that there was nothing to worry about, so I hadn't given it much thought.

I now know that the clot had not broken down sufficiently to allow proper blood flow and, in the matter of a few hours, his foot had turned black and swollen.

Trying not to panic, I rang the local surgery. Within half an hour an out-of-hours doctor arrived. Looking back, I now realise Dad was feverish and unaware of what was going on. That was a blessing for him and meant he didn't tune in to my sense of horror at what was happening.

Was I over-reacting? Evidently not. We didn't usually ride in ambulances (that would be too much drama for my family). Yet, the doctor was ordering one, and Dad was whisked into the nearby Torbay hospital to be prodded and poked before falling into a restless sleep.

I sat with him through that night, worrying myself sick. Thankfully, my brother appeared in response to my frantic call and reassured me I hadn't gone over the top.

Dad had gone from laughing and joking to seriously ill in just a few hours. We were trying hard to make sense of what was happening.

****

For the last three weeks Dad had been languishing on a small ward, gradually eating less, and losing interest in the world outside.

The events of 9/11 came as a distraction because his situation was deteriorating dramatically. His doctors, unable to save the dead limb, had decided to remove his right foot.

My father was self-administering morphine after the operation, but it seemed as if the doctors were waiting for something more to happen. The insertion of a feeding tube that day added to our anguish and his pain.

Once again, we were uninformed; knowledge is power, but we didn't yet know how to get adequate information as we still had no access to the internet. My brother and I were swept along on the tide that is hospital daily life.

Thankfully, I spent most of that time sitting with Dad in the hospital. With hindsight, I see it as a precious gift.

Staying in his house, I was surrounded by the details of his life and my family memories.

A week after the events of 9/11, an early morning phone call re-focused my mind.

'Your father is very sick this morning, and you need to get here as soon as possible,' the nurse said.

'OK, OK,' I stammered. Shocked by the abrupt awakening, I rang my brother.

'Steve, Dad's bad. See you there.' I was brief and to the point, as tears threatened.

After a headlong dash, we arrived together at his bedside to find him looking terrified and gasping for breath. He was surrounded by nurses and a doctor who took us aside.

'Your father is an extremely sick man and will die very soon. His system is full of poison, and his organs have already begun to shut down.'

Stark and to the point, this man was used to giving bad news, but we weren't used to receiving it. My brother grasped me in a wretched hug, both of us shocked. We had no words to express our feelings.

While they took him down to Intensive Care, we were offered a cup of tea, the British comfort for any situation, before going down to spend the last few hours of my sixty-six-year-old dad's life, watching his body shut down.

'Can I kiss him?' I asked, almost afraid to touch him as the last breath of his life rattled out of his body

'Of course, Dawne. He knows you are here,' replied the nurse. Watching her holding his head and talking to him, easing his way out of this life, I was shocked to my core. How could this be happening?

I managed my kiss, looking into his milky eyes, clouded with death. I hope he felt that soft goodbye, wanting to keep him with me but realising he was almost gone. I had never seen anyone die before. I feel now that it was a privilege to share that with him, but it was probably the hardest moment of my life.

'I can see them,' he whispered. Later, I realised he was being welcomed by his family on the "other side".

****

He died of a Pulmonary Embolism; a blood clot that had travelled from his leg to his lung. There, I have finally admitted it to myself. It was the clot that killed him, and it makes me want to cry just to think of it. We were so close, especially in his final weeks, yet I was powerless to help him on his final journey as I sat watching his life ebb away. It could have been such a different story if I had known then what I know now.

****

CHAPTER TWO
It Seemed Like a Good Idea at the Time

Groaning loudly as I eased off my sweaty back brace, I was ready to burst into tears. Flinging two sturdy walking poles aside, I hobbled over to a canvas chair to assess the damage to my trek ravaged boots.

Whatever had possessed me to undertake this challenge when I could have been at home in Mallorca, taking it easy in the winter sunshine? Not camping out in the harsh and challenging wilderness of the Sahara Desert. It had been an exceptionally long day's slog through the soft, dragging sand of the dunes, and I was mentally and physically exhausted.

Entering camp twelve weary hours after our early start, the light was fading quickly as the velvety darkness of the night closed in around us.

Bringing up the rear, I was last to arrive, accompanied by the medic and our local trek leader, watchful as ever that we were all shepherded into the safety of our tents. What was I doing in the dunes of eastern Morocco?

****

Ten months previously it had seemed like a good idea but, as with many such plans, I had been carried along on a wave of enthusiasm. Actually, that and a warm feeling of camaraderie with Sarah, an old school friend. She isn't old, our friendship is.

About forty years ago, when we were both irreverent but relatively well-behaved sixteen-year-olds, my dad lost his job with little warning, and the family regrouped and made a quick move southward.

Bristol seemed to be a possibility, with cheaper living and property costs. We promptly sold our "up and coming executive" detached house in a secluded close in Solihull and moved on, scarcely pausing for breath to look back and wonder quite what had happened.

However, our move was due to take place just after Christmas, a few short months before I was due to sit O Level exams, the equivalent of today's GCSEs.

A change of location, school and exam board could prove to be potentially disastrous for me. What was to be done?

The word went out from school. Would any family be prepared to take me in as a lodger for those few months? Quite a question.

Recently, Sarah explained to me that she went home and asked her mum and dad, 'Can I have a sister?' After much deliberation between our parents, an offer duly appeared from them and, only a day after Christmas, I moved my few possessions into their home, and waved a tearful goodbye to my family.

Our exploits over the following six months sharply defined our differences. At that time, my short, dark-haired friend was harder to get to know. Her ever-present smile was the front she presented to the world. My outgoing personality was, as yet, undamaged by life's brickbats, in complete contrast to her more measured ways.

Thoughtful and kind, Sarah had inherited these attributes from her parents, who took me into their home and looked after me in exactly the same way they cared for their only child.

Their patience and support knew no bounds, and I am sure I tested them to the limit. I don't know what they had expected when I turned up on their doorstep.

We had not been close friends before I exploded into their lives, so they knew nothing of my background.

It would seem that I was the one to lead their daughter astray, but it was her determination that got us through those difficult times.

They were happy and productive months, living with Sarah and her parents while we both sat our exams with, I am relieved to say, better than expected results. So, in between the Youth Club, experimenting with face packs and frequent visits to the local swimming pool, we had managed to do some studying.

We would wander into Chelsea Girl, a famous store in 1976, eager to try on the tight-fitting flared trousers and cheesecloth tops we yearned to wear while singing along to the glam rock songs that were blaring out over the sound system.

Slade was a favourite band of ours, especially as they were from Birmingham. However, I was more likely to be found shaking my long hair and "getting down" to "Caroline" by Status Quo. I quite fancied myself as a young rocker.

Of course, I got the blame for our extra-curricular activities and, I have to admit, the face packs had been my idea. I had never used one, and we both had a keen interest in clothes and makeup, quite late in the day compared to today's teenagers.

One Saturday afternoon, we were shopping in town, and I suggested we go into Boots and inspect the tempting displays of cosmetics we were eager to try out. We weren't allowed makeup at school and had little use for it at our church Youth Club.

With the benefit of hindsight, it seems to me that the 1970s was a gentler and happier time, at least for us as teenagers. We didn't appear to have the worries and stresses of today's young people, but maybe we were just lucky and had loving families looking out for us.

'OK, Sarah, you can blame me for this one,' I teased, wanting to get adventurous. My friend quite happily joined in, choosing a mud-based face pack for me.

'Yuk! I'm not smearing my face with mud for anyone,' she muttered, rummaging around on the shelves of our local branch of Boots the Chemist.

'Do you know what an avocado is?' It might sound odd, but they were not commonly available in the 1970s, at least not in our part of Birmingham.

'No idea,' I chuckled, so we chose an avocado based "gloop" for her.

Later that evening, we disappeared into her bedroom and began to experiment. I guess it was the fit of giggles erupting from the room that brought her mother upstairs.

My memory is that she was quite cross with us, but, naturally, we thought it hilarious. Probably the mess on the blankets and in the bathroom proved sufficient to provoke the anger, her mum unmoved by mumbled apologies and covert giggles.

We were "partners in crime" and loved to experiment outside of school. However, in class we each had our own group of friends and in the playground we didn't mix.

I spent most of my time learning to play backgammon "like a pro", sneaking around to the boys' side of the school at lunch and break times, trying to outplay the lad I had nagged into teaching me the rules.

Sarah followed other pursuits but, back at her house, we were twins pretty much intent on sending her mum to an early grave.

At the end of my stay, exams over and the whole summer to look forward to, we said heartfelt and tearful goodbyes as I climbed into my dad's car for the trip south to Bristol.

My friend came down for a couple of visits to my new home but, after several years of exchanged birthday cards and presents, we had both moved on in quite different directions.

If social networking sites or Skype had been available, our friendship might have continued, but phone calls were expensive, and, as for letters, we were teenagers. We had no time for snail mail.

There was no good reason why we drifted apart. We had been so close but, being typically self-involved teenagers looking only to the future, we eventually lost touch altogether.

Friends Re-united was the forerunner of Facebook and, in the early internet days, it was a way of renewing old friendships. Inputting schools and clubs, it enabled others who had signed up to make cautious contact. Not as immediate as Facebook, it felt safe to use, so you can imagine my excitement when I opened my account one day to find a contact message from Sarah.

It was at least twenty-five years since we had been in touch. It was a real blast from the past and I felt quite unsure of what to expect from the message which was asking if I was 'That Dawn with an e who lived with Sarah Plowman in 1976?'

That aroused all sorts of emotions and memories, ranging from excitement and anticipation to worry about what was to come next. I hastily typed a reply.

'Yes, that's me. I don't know where to start. There is so much to catch up on. You go first.' I was too shocked to be able to think about what to say next, and I suppose I hoped Sarah would lead the way.

Over the next few weeks, we re-established contact, excited to hear each other's news after so long. There was so much to say. Messages flew back and forth, full of details about how life had progressed for each of us since we were last in touch: marriages (two; one each), divorces (also two; one each), children and parents all came into the mix.

Saddest of all was having to tell her that my dad had been dead for several years. She had got to know him quite well, and I knew that her parents, into their 70s by then, would take that news badly.

He had been the driving force behind my stay with the family, visiting me weekly during that time. He was the enduring figure in all our memories.

Most of all, I wanted to express my profound gratitude for the support and love I had received from Sarah and her parents during what was a challenging time for me and my family. I was, and still am, very keen to cherish our relationship this time around, based on mutual liking and respect, rather than the frantic friendships of our teenage years.

Our first face-to-face meeting was a short visit to my home in Mallorca. Her eldest daughter, Charlie, had made the arrangements and came over too.

I felt my friend's apprehension about the person she would find.

As a teenager, I had been full of energy and confidence, ready to go out and conquer the world, which made me a force to be reckoned with. Sarah had borne the brunt of my boisterous and sometimes commanding personality with fortitude but was I still the same?

I don't think we stopped talking in those all too brief couple of days. Charlie was a welcome foil between us as raw emotions were poked and prodded in our catch up.

'I can just imagine what you two were like as teenagers,' she laughed, a strong character yet willing to sit on the side lines as her mother and I babbled away. 'A right pair of tearaways.'

'Hardly,' I replied, thinking of today's far more aggressive style of teenage angst. 'We were quite angelic,' I commented, tongue firmly in cheek.

'You were very bossy though,' laughed Sarah, glass of red wine in hand. I couldn't hope to disagree with that statement. I was. My resolve then and there was to be more of the person I had become over the past twenty-five years: altogether gentler with an aptitude for listening. Unless, of course, I am excited about something, in which case I am as noisy and bossy as ever.

Thank goodness for Charlie's calming influence; she made a good umpire.

****

'Please come over and visit and make it soon because Dad's not so good. It's October now, but I'm afraid he may not be around even at Christmas.'

Sarah managed to persuade me it was time to go and visit my temporary family.

The evident fragility of her father and the desire to express in person my thanks for all they had done for me, combined to get me onto a plane within the month. It was a hectic and emotional couple of days with kids and grandkids rounded up for me to meet.

'Do you think I've changed much?' I asked my friend, dreading her reply. I hadn't had the nerve to ask that question when we first met up again.

'Oh no,' she replied. 'We haven't changed a bit. Well, we're both a bit blonder now, but that's our prerogative as we get older.'

Between the family reunion and reminiscing, we found time for ourselves and had quite a discussion about our plans, goals and things we would like to achieve.

'I enjoy hiking around Mallorca. In the spring and autumn I often join a group and do a decent walk on a Sunday.'

'That's interesting,' replied Sarah. 'I've just started doing a similar thing with a good mate. We went out to the Malvern Hills recently, and the scenery is spectacular.'

'That's a coincidence. Our crowd were talking about doing some sort of a trek for charity,' I sighed wistfully, thinking of Comic Relief, somewhat scaled down. 'I wouldn't mind trying something like that.'

I had travelled extensively in the previous few years, both for work and pleasure. Package holidays, backpacking adventures and road trips; you name it, I had tried it. I have a strong sense of curiosity that drives me to visit unusual and out-of-the-way places, including parts of Nepal, Africa and South America. However, those destinations were often not my choice, being dictated by the whims of employers and friends alike.

I had also started getting involved with the Lions Club charity to channel some of my enthusiasm for organising events as part of a team. However, I was becoming frustrated with committees.

The media bombards us with sponsored activities these days, and I was starting to take note, forming a vague desire to be a part of that.

'Oh, me too,' came the reply that was to change our immediate future.

There it was: the germ of an idea, a challenge and it seemed like a good idea at the time...

Only a few days later, I received an e-mail from Sarah, asking if I had been serious about a trek.

For the next couple of months, we dared and double-dared each other into our madcap escapade, but how daring would we be?

'Do you fancy a parachute jump?' I asked, just to tease. We had already dismissed that because we were, by our own admission, scaredy cats. Rock climbing and similar pursuits were also disregarded.

Lacking both balance and coordination, it seemed best that I had both feet firmly planted on the ground for this caper.

It had to be a trek as neither of us was keen on cycling, preferring to view scenery on foot. So that wasn't an issue.

However, we both had a burning desire to get involved with the wave of media directed fundraising by completing some kind of a physical challenge. Madcap? It was for us.

Sarah describes herself as 'A middle-aged nan with a dream, who has never attempted anything like this.'

My life had been a series of adventures in recent years. Yet, I always seemed to follow someone else's dream, be it a friend's desire to go sailing or a driving trip in South America in a group of strong-minded people, all intent on seeing their favourite sights.

This one would be specifically mine; a trek because that was within my comfort zone and driven by a desire to fundraise for my chosen charity: Thrombosis UK.

I would be in charge of this particular aspect of my destiny, which appealed to me, coupled with a sense that joining my old school friend in such an enterprise would cement our newly reformed relationship.

****

Christmas festivities were over, and other things were uppermost in my mind until, one January evening, my computer started ringing. Skype was trying to attract my attention.

'Have you decided yet? Time is moving on. It's almost February already.'

Sarah and I communicated mainly by e-mails, to keep phone costs down as she was based in England, and I lived in Spain. We had very different schedules to our day, and England is an hour behind Spain, so it wasn't that easy to make time for chats. E-mails could be sent late at night after the day's chores were finished, and we had time to think, plot and plan. This Skype call had to come.

She had managed to get me to focus on our plan, and we had discussed various options without committing to anything.

I had decided that my mate should choose our destination. We were spoiled for choice. However, she had never travelled outside of Europe before.

We both knew we wanted to walk (I don't do bikes. My lack of coordination and dodgy balance contribute to the disaster that is me on a bicycle), so had only contacted those companies that organise treks as charity fundraisers.

'I've seen something which might suit us, and I really want to do it,' blurted an excited Sarah, a few days later.

That put me on the spot. I had less and less wiggle room as options narrowed down, and she pushed for a commitment to one challenge or another. Alarm bells were ringing in my head. Was I getting into something I may not be up to, either physically or mentally?

Then in my fifties, I tried to keep fit and active with an outdoor life, but my body was suffering the ravages of time. I know that sounds dramatic. However, in the previous twenty years, I had both shoulders operated on for broken tendons, one knee cleaned out and suffered from intermittent back strain. I was far from being a flexible and dynamic youngster, although I tried not to let that stop me from doing anything I wanted to do.

'We can go to eastern Morocco in November and trek through the Sahara Desert.'

That got me motivated. I have a passion for deserts. That probably sounds weird, but we are all moved by something, be it cities, rolling countryside, mountains, lakes or the sea. In my case, it happens to be deserts with huge skies and endless vistas, seemingly empty, with vast oceans of slowly shifting sand dunes. Possibly even a masterful and sultry Berber chief, galloping on a wild stallion, appearing out of a shimmering mirage.

My heart began to race as my imagination ran amok. Sarah could not have come up with a suggestion more likely to get me involved and motivated.

'We won't have to deal with jet lag, you won't need those horrible injections you use on long flights and

36

altitude won't be an issue.' Crikey, she had thought it all out, but why were they even considerations at all?

****

Shortly after Dad died, I visited my doctor.

'We have the results of your blood tests, Dawne. You have Factor Five Leiden, a clotting disorder, inherited from your father.'

She explained that this gene mutation means, in any circumstance where clotting is possible, I am much more likely to suffer. So, for example, postoperatively everyone is vulnerable, due to being immobile, me more so.

I had continued asking questions, and now, some months later, this was my diagnosis.

Going back into the family history, sudden death had been a frequent pattern with Dad's relatives, and his mother had suffered a blood clot in childbirth.

I was still woefully ignorant about the subject and barely knew what questions to ask.

In recent years, I have had more tests that show I have inherited Factor V Leiden from both parents, a double whammy. In some cases, I am eighty-eight (yes, 88) times more at risk than someone who does not have this gene mutation.

Whilst my dad died of a blood clot, my mother has never had an issue. She is in her 80s, keeps fit and eats healthily. Just because you have a clotting disorder, it doesn't mean you will automatically have a thrombosis.

It is a complex subject that I cannot claim to understand fully, but I have found this particular charity to be a reliable source of relevant information.

Thrombosis UK (formerly known as Lifeblood: The Thrombosis Charity) is a small organisation, achieving remarkable things with few resources.

For more details, go to their website:
www.thrombosisuk.org

Their aim is education and research, as well as support for anyone affected by any clotting issue (and there are many variations).

Their website is packed full of facts, links and survivor stories. With few paid employees, most of the impetus for the work of the charity comes from volunteers who range through the entire spectrum of health professionals.

Whilst research is vital, their primary aim is to ensure that clinicians at every level can diagnose blood clots which are notoriously difficult to spot because often there are no visible symptoms at all.

Sarah chose to support Breakthrough Breast Cancer as she had a friend undergoing treatment for that disease. It is a large organisation, with good contacts, a thriving fundraising operation and agreements already in place with challenge companies which made it simple for her to sign up as a fundraiser.

Having become aware of Thrombosis UK, and the work it does in education, support and research, I was keen to help. Consequently, I had many conversations with them about my plans to raise money for them.

The cause is important to me, not only in memory of Dad but more especially because I am a survivor. I want to show there can be life after blood clots. It can be active, challenging and the risks are manageable.

Trustees of the charity were informed of my plans, and they contacted Charity Challenge so that I could do my trek.

The reaction of the trustees can be summed up in the words of one of their members who said that, should I want to do this for them, I should be given as much encouragement and support as possible and a medal too.

****

By February we had settled on our challenge and our charities. With a joint shiver of anticipation, we had signed on the dotted line. In a mere eight months, we were to trek through the Sahara Desert in eastern Morocco for our respective charities: Breakthrough Breast Cancer and Thrombosis UK.

"Partners in crime" again? Not really but certainly the two of us had a joint purpose and motivation to embark on such an adventure together. We were on our way.

CHAPTER THREE
Fundraising

'Hi Joan, how are you? Three bags full of stuff? Blimey, you've been having a clear out.'

'Can you collect them today?' asked Joan, a close friend who had donated lots of her unwanted household items in response to my requests for things to sell to raise funds for Thrombosis UK.

'Of course I can. How about a quick lunch while we're at it?'

'OK. See you around one o'clock,' she replied, brief and to the point as always.

'Not more things to store,' grumbled Bernie, my long-suffering partner. Our garage was gradually filling up with donated "stuff" for the car boot sale coming up the following weekend.

'Can't stop to chat, too busy.' I flung this over my shoulder whilst getting into our very handy van to go and make my collection, with a nice chatty lunch as a bonus.

A couple of weeks before this, I had rung another friend called Hazel. Having retired from the retail business, she seemed like a good person to ask about selling "stuff".

'Five o'clock in the morning? Really?' My disbelieving response to a question about car boot sales. 'You queued up from five o'clock in the morning to get a pitch?'

'No, I haven't been to this particular market,' replied Hazel. 'But I have it on good authority that four o'clock would ensure we get a decent spot,' she added, groaning at the mere thought of it.

Shocked? You bet I was. I only recognise one five o'clock and that is just before gin o'clock. Dawne may be my name, but it is not my favourite time of day. However, I had to bow to the superior knowledge and experience of Hazel, who had done a few similar markets in the past. I was just a lowly car boot sale virgin.

We had both enjoyed planning our stall (during our stints as volunteers at the local Lions Club charity shop) and collecting things generously donated, but realities were starting to hit home. An early start it would be.

Fundraising is no easy matter, particularly in the current economic climate. It is all very well sending out "that" e-mail to all your contacts, politely asking for donations to your cause. The secret is to reach a wider circle of people, and that is far easier said than done.

If you have celebrity connections or friends in the entertainment industry, things evolve from offers of help, perhaps with musicians getting together for an evening of fun and frolics. However, no celebrities were hiding in my address book.

I did not always want to rely on other people to raise funds. To do various events on my own (or with Hazel) seemed to be the way forward.

However, charity begins at home. I started by paying all the expenses myself so that every penny donated would go to Thrombosis UK. It cost much the same as a week in a nice hotel somewhere interesting, and, whilst this would not be a holiday (far from it), it would certainly satisfy my curiosity about the Sahara Desert, the subject of much speculation over the past months.

How much was I willing to go through to raise these funds? The exertion of the trek aside, getting up in the middle of the night to go car booting seemed like an appropriate level of sacrifice; I like my sleep.

As I switched off my alarm clock, long before it was due to go off, I noticed Hazel's regal-looking cat staring at me from their hallway. No doubt it was wondering at the sight of a bleary-eyed woman blundering about in the dark, trying to get dressed without waking the entire household.

I could hear my friend moving around and followed her downstairs to the kitchen, where we exchanged grumbles about not having slept, waiting for the alarm to go off.

She had kindly invited me to stay that night as her house was nearer to the market site. We had enjoyed a relaxed evening with her husband, sitting outside on their terrace in the warm spring evening air and musing about the coming day while trying not to imbibe too much wine. Hangovers were the last thing we needed.

We dispensed with pleasantries, decided to forgo breakfast, and climbed wearily into my van, which was already full. It was three o'clock in the morning, and we had barely slept.

'What time is it now?' I asked some time later, trying not to sound petulant and manifestly failing.

'Half past six, and it looks like there is some movement up ahead,' replied Hazel, far perkier than me for that time of day.

We had been in an unmoving queue for a pitch since four o'clock, snuggled up in the comparative warmth of my battered van.

Having spent the previous few weeks collecting whatever items friends and acquaintances were willing to donate, we were about to find out if they would sell.

We had everything from water skis and rugs to clothes and assorted bric-a-brac, so I was sure something would appeal to our potential buyers.

'Did you remember the sun umbrellas?' I asked. Our one concern was how hot it was going to be.

May is a lovely time in Mallorca, sunny without the fierce heat of the summer months, but standing out bareheaded in full sun was not an option for either of us. Silly hats (actually a cool hat for Hazel and a daft one for me; she was a milliner by trade) and sun umbrellas were mandatory.

A bewildering clamour of instructions came from all directions in both Spanish and English as I tried to carefully squeeze the van into one car length of space, between stalls already set up with traders hard at work.

'Back another metre, no forwards, and turn the wheel to the right. More. Go on! Oh, mind the stall on the left. Yes! That will do,' yelled Hazel. 'That was amazing. I would have burst into tears and gone home by now,' she confessed.

All that, added to the buyers milling around the back of our van the moment we had parked, meant our arrival had proved quite stressful.

Thank goodness Hazel was wise to the ways of such things. After her previous outings, she was well versed in the mayhem that can start as clothes and bric-a-brac appear from the cluttered depths of crammed bags and boxes.

'Don't make eye contact,' she ordered, aware that she was likely to get a rude reply if she got too bossy with me, but I felt out of my depth and was willing to follow her lead.

'Let them wait until we're ready,' she added as we watched the grasping hands, eager to grab things from us.

We eventually cleared away all the hangers-on, carefully set up our tables, sun umbrellas and rails and then stuck close together.

Donated items were grabbed quickly in the first hour of our day. Men were pawing over heaps of books and bric-a-brac while women clutched at jewellery and clothes, all firing requests for lower prices at us as we struggled to keep control of goods sold and those being merely handled.

Two hectic hours after our arrival, Hazel was happily tidying our already ravaged stall.

'What time is it now then?' Gosh, I can be a pain sometimes, and Hazel would only agree.

'Nine o'clock in the morning.'

'I should still be in my bed,' I grumbled. 'We've already sold heaps, and now it's gone quiet.' I was beginning to wonder if we could go home, but I knew we wouldn't. We had to stick it out to raise as much money as we could.

After that, sales became a little slower but steady. We were learning the most easily saleable things for future reference, jewellery being favourite, but also the hardest to keep track of in the melee.

'I wonder if anything small has been slipped into a bag without us noticing,' Hazel mused. 'It's a job to know who is planning to buy,' she added, still somehow managing to look cool in the steadily rising temperatures.

A lover of linen, my friend always appeared stylish even in the most trying of situations, while I, with three-quarter length trousers topped with an increasingly dusty charity t-shirt, looked my usual scruffy self.

Much as she might try, I don't think Hazel will ever convert me to her elegant ways. She had, however, taught me well, and I could now spot designer clothing I would have passed by some months before.

We took time to survey the scene and the frenetic activity on the dusty patch of land. Our pitch was opposite the municipal car pound, and we watched trucks busy towing any car whose owner was rash enough to ignore the parking restrictions on market day.

The regular stallholders had already taken all the best pitches, close to the car park where everyone had to pass by. As casuals, we were relegated to a location on the furthest outer edge of the huge industrial estate.

Not everyone would get to us, but things were busy, the sun was already rising high into the cloudless sky, and the gentle breeze was whirling up dust eddies on the rough ground.

My stomach rumbled as the mouth-watering smell of bacon frying drifted past our noses. It contrasted sharply with the water and dry biscuits we had brought with us and competed with the stink of rotting food from the bins not far away.

We hadn't known what to expect but realised it might not be easy to leave the stall at any time. That meant toilet visits would be infrequent, and there would be no chance to go and find yummy things to eat.

We were busy concentrating on our patch, watching all the time for light fingers, lifting small items of jewellery and bric-a-brac to look at, ensuring they were either bought and paid for or returned to the stall.

Although we were hot and dusty, we had a lot of fun, bartering and arguing over various items. I hadn't expected to enjoy myself so much.

Car boot sales are notorious for low prices and customers wanting things even cheaper. We needed to sell as much as possible, so let clothing, in particular, go for whatever we could get, even designer shirts, although Hazel hung on for 5€ whenever possible.

Now and again, a cheeky customer would get away with a bargain, but it was all part of the game. However, surly or rude people raised our hackles, and we proved worthy adversaries.

I even received a round of applause after one particularly fraught bargaining session, which gradually descended into farce; I was *not* going to let these guys have a pair of skirts for 3€.

The banter went to and fro, with me intent on sticking to my guns.

'Best price 5€ for the pair,' I countered their latest offer.

'No, 3€.'

'5€, for charity,' I insisted, holding tightly onto the gypsy style, flouncy skirts in question.

'3€.' They wouldn't budge on the price and were moving closer to me in a positively threatening manner, hands outstretched and shouting at the tops of their voices.

'No, get away with you! 5€.' I yelled back at top volume with lots of laughs, but they were becoming aggressive, and I didn't like that.

Eventually, they gave up and moved on, giving me the chance to take a bow to the assembled crowd, who were delightedly watching our antics. Enjoying the round of applause and laughter, I could finally breathe a sigh of relief. I am pleased to report that the skirts later went for 3€ each.

It was hard when my personal items came under scrutiny. The pretty necklace that had cost £20 some years ago was now only worth 2€, or the much-loved dress, which I had grown out of long ago, described as

'A bit dull isn't it? I'll take it off your hands for a euro.' It didn't do my ego much good when a couple of teenagers laughed at a pair of shorts I used to think were quite funky.

By one o'clock we were done; hot, tired, thirsty and desperately in need of a wee.

By now, our pitch was in full sun, and we were glad of the shade from our umbrellas, hats and sunglasses. Without them, we would have fried.

Dust devils danced around the scrubby ground, swirling in our hair, mingling with the sweat and sun lotion on our faces and in all those important little places.

'Let's pack up and get away from here. I need a baguette and a nice cool shandy,' I suggested.

'I need a wee first,' replied Hazel emphatically.

By then, we were both cross-legged. We had been rationing the water whilst attempting to keep hydrated in the heat.

Knowing "wee time" was near, we gulped down the last lukewarm dregs and raced to the toilets, pushing aside anyone hanging around in our hurry for relief. Thank goodness there wasn't a queue.

In a nearby café, we retired to an empty table, covered in the abandoned remains of a snack, where we had time to review our morning.

'I think we've done OK,' said Hazel.

'Well, we won't know until I've been home and counted out the pennies,' I replied. 'That is where I am off to pronto. I'm going to enjoy this shandy first, though. I'm parched.'

Arriving home, I left my van, still full of our remaining booty, parked on the driveway where it stayed all night. Meanwhile, I lugged the heavy cash box into the cool and quiet house. It was three o'clock, a full twelve hours since we had awoken from our paltry three hours of sleep.

After our hectic morning of car booting, I was shattered. I crashed out on the sofa and fell asleep within minutes.

A couple of hours later, still feeling very weary, I rang Hazel to tell her our news. I was relieved she was already awake, although sounding tired.

'You will never guess how much we made,' I teased.

'Oh, go on. I reckon around 100€.'

'It's much more than that. It's 160€.'

'Wow! That was so worthwhile, and I enjoyed it, even if I am completely worn out. Shall we do it again sometime?'

Hazel was as thrilled as I was and very keen to repeat the whole process. It was a great start to my fundraising; not in itself a large amount but significant enough to us.

We did another four sales over the next year, thoroughly enjoying ourselves in the process. It is a demanding way of earning a relatively small sum of money but, as it only cost us 6€ for the pitch, we considered it to be time well spent.

Each outing was also an opportunity to spread the word. Most car booters were not in the least bit interested in Thrombosis UK. However, each time I was approached by people who had been affected by blood clots and wanted to know more.

It helps to talk through your experience with other survivors, and I was fully kitted out with leaflets, website addresses and lots of other useful information, and I learned something new from almost everyone I spoke to.

Fundraising is vital to assist the work of any charity but for me, the emphasis has always been on spreading the word about the dangers of clots, how to spot them, how to avoid them and where to get support.

One of our more compact car boot sale stalls.

Chatting over a market stall can do that, and I have found that everyone who has had a thrombosis feels a deep need to talk about it. Often family members can't or won't discuss what happened and comparing stories with a fellow sufferer can be a great source of comfort and relief.

Helping out at the local Lions Club charity shop brought me into contact with lots of people, many of whom also donated to Thrombosis UK.

Next door to the shop was a lovely little café, run by a fabulous lady called Rebecca who offered the idea of having a Coffee Morning in support of the charity. I didn't need asking twice.

I couldn't wait to get to work on the details, inviting anyone in my address book that I thought might like to come along.

As the date drew near, Hazel helped me pick through our remaining car boot sale donations to find some suitable items to sell on the day. Rebecca was so generous with her time and her wonderful cakes that I knew we were onto a winning morning.

The early September day dawned bright and sunny, and the cafe was open, with a mouth-watering display of cakes smelling delicious.

Hazel and I had set up a table of books and videos plus another laden down with eye-catching jewellery and makeup items.

I was dressed in my trekking gear and ready to answer questions about my Sahara adventure. I had no time to feel nervous as people started to arrive.

Raffle tickets were selling well. Meanwhile, I was posing for the press.

Ready for the Coffee Morning at Mama's.

'That's it. A shot just in front of the cafe, Dawne,' chivvied the photographer who was recording the event.

'I'll use your write up to go with it,' he said as he rushed away to get his copy sent off.

The more coverage the better, and I was gradually getting recognised in my local area as "the lady walking through the desert".

Wendy Peters, a journalist at the Daily Bulletin (our island-wide English newspaper), mentioned me several times in her column, which certainly helped to spread the word.

There were lots of friends gathered outside in the sunshine, catching up on gossip and picking through our tables of goodies. Some passers-by even stopped to ask about the trek and, finding out that it was for charity, pressed cash into my hot, sticky hands for Thrombosis UK.

It had been a busy morning, and it was some time before Rebecca poked her head around the kitchen door and asked if there were any more plates to wash, as I headed into the café to lend a hand.

'No, all done.' I gave her a heartfelt hug, appreciating how much effort it had taken her to make the event such a great success as I counted out the money to cover her costs.

'See you soon. I'll give you a call when I know exactly how much we've raised.'

As I drove home, I reviewed the morning and decided it had all been worthwhile. The cakes had been delicious while the customers enjoyed the get-together and spent their euros on trinkets while asking me lots of questions. It just remained for me to count the cash.

As the sum mounted up, I began to feel excited. I grabbed the phone and called Rebecca as soon as I knew the results of all our efforts.

'Go on, how much did we raise?'

'Can you believe it? We made 260€,' I blurted.

'Really?' she yelled, delightedly. 'That's a lot from a three-hour Coffee Morning.'

'Yes,' I replied. 'It was your coffee and cakes that brought people together. There were several cash donations too. I am amazed it has amounted to so much.'

'Me too,' said Rebecca. 'Well done you.'

'Oh no, not me – it was you who offered to organise the event in the first place. You made it happen. I just can't thank you enough.'

I was overjoyed. Thanks, Rebecca, it made all your efforts worthwhile.

The Coffee Morning had more repercussions than I had bargained for as I met her partner Ian Pickles who ran the local ballroom dance school.

Having heard that they often had "Not So Strictly!" dance competitions (their version of Strictly Come Dancing), with a charity raffle, on the spur of the moment I approached him.

'Is there any chance you would consider running one of your raffles for Thrombosis UK?' I cheekily asked.

'Hmmm, yes,' he replied, grinning. 'There is one condition though.'

'What have you got in mind?' I answered, thinking it couldn't be anything too dreadful. More fool me.

'You have to agree to compete,' said Ian.

'What, me? Ballroom dancing?' I gasped, being more suited to trekking boots and hiking trousers than glitz and glamorous dresses.

'Yes, you. It's good fun and a great way to get fit,' he reassured me. 'I'll give you some free lessons. We only need to practise for a short time beforehand to keep things from getting too serious. It's meant to be fun.'

What could I do but agree?

Oh dear, what had I done?

Fundraising can be very humbling. People are so generous, and donations can come from the most unexpected sources.

Picture this: a drinks party on the terrace of a house high above the spectacular port of Andratx in the south of Mallorca.

You might justifiably think that this should be party time and not a good moment for fundraising. Yes, sometimes the trek, Thrombosis UK, and the money had to be left at home, mainly to give my long-suffering friends a break. However, people I hadn't met before didn't get away without at least a quick resume of my plans.

It was one of those hot, sticky August nights when all you can do is sit outside and drink cool beers or cocktails.

I was introduced to a lady called Desi who seemed interested in my reasons for supporting Thrombosis UK. I wasn't about to let her go easily and had been enthusiastically bombarding her with information about my plans.

'I will give you 500,' said Desi.

'500 what?' Had I heard her correctly? I wasn't sure as I had half an ear on a joke being told on the opposite side of the terrace.

'500 pounds of course,' she replied.

'Really?' was my disbelieving response. I was now paying close attention.

'Yes. Take my business card and keep sending me e-mails until you get a reply. I'll sort it out when I get home,' she instructed.

I could hardly believe what I had heard. £500 was a big deal to me and a massive boost to my funds.

Desi proved to be the star of our evening. Larger than life and full of anecdotes, she was good fun and very interesting too. Without giving much away about herself or her life, she joined in the travel stories and joke-telling with gusto.

I was somewhat befuddled by now, as the cocktails were liberally circulated, and on an empty stomach too, which is never a good idea.

'It's probably the wine talking,' I thought, tucking the card into my handbag and sashaying on unaccustomed high heels into the lounge for pizza, wine and more jokes.

Examining my aching head at home the following morning for any evidence of bad behaviour, I cringed. Had I really collared Desi and bombarded her with tales of trekking and fundraising plans?

'I don't think you said too much,' reassured Bernie. 'You only sat with her for about half an hour, and she was telling jokes most of the night.'

I was relieved. There can only have been a short time for me to get in on the conversation.

'I can't believe it. I think she has agreed to donate £500.' I tried to dig into the depths of my addled brain to remember exactly what had been said.

'Why not send her an e-mail and see if you get a reply,' replied Bernie sagely.

'Hey, guess what? I just googled Desi, and she only has an MBE for services to equestrianism, including some major fundraising. Oh, how embarrassing. She has raised enormous amounts of money, in between training Olympic standard dressage horses.'

I felt mortified, afraid that I might have come across as self-absorbed, with a paltry target of £1,000 for my fundraising.

'Don't be silly,' said Bernie. 'She can obviously spot a winner, in the enclosure or out of it.'

Her offer had given me a boost, and I felt great for days afterwards.

Two weeks later, I went online to check my Trekker Girl Just Giving account.

'She's done it!' I shouted from the office. 'Desi's only gone and donated that £500, and I've smashed my target.' I was elated.

I immediately e-mailed Thrombosis UK as I was so overwhelmed, bubbling with excitement. I couldn't stop smiling.

Not only did Desi offer support, but she also made me feel humble in the face of such generosity and gave me greater belief in myself.

Sarah was also on top of the world, having received news of a £500 donation from her employer. We were going to be happy trekkers.

It would take another book to mention all the people who so generously donated to my fund, showing confidence in my ability to achieve such a goal. I hadn't expected that.

They have all given help, not only financially, but in so many other ways, such as printing leaflets, donating items for sale or giving their time to help me fundraise.

www.justgiving.com/trekkergirl is my donations page and serves as a good reminder of all the assistance I have been given.

One of the greatest gifts has to be the moral support I have received. I could not achieve anything in a vacuum, and both family and friends proved themselves more than equal to the task.

On my next visit to see the family, I was approached by Jodi, Bernie's twelve-year-old granddaughter, who had some money scrunched into the palm of her hand.

'It's for you, for your charity,' she coyly explained.

'You are a star,' I murmured, cuddling her. She had just given her pocket money to Thrombosis UK.

'It's not much,' she replied.

'As Tesco says, "Every little helps",' I replied, almost moved to tears and delighted that she wanted to support the cause. The saying, "Charity begins at home" really does hold true.

CHAPTER FOUR
Mallorca Boot Camp

'Blimey, I thought September would be cooler than this. My phone shows thirty degrees,' exclaimed a hot and sweaty Sarah. 'What's that in old money?' she puffed, out of breath. 'You know I still think in feet and inches.'

'Oh, that's nearly ninety degrees,' I quickly calculated. 'You could fry an egg on this tarmac. Too much information I know, but I'm sweating from places I didn't know I had.'

Our training was going well then.

Sarah had decided to take a week's holiday from work and join me in Mallorca to train together for our upcoming trek. Up until then, we had only been out on our own or in the company of other friends. It would be our first chance to compare notes together.

'Even my socks are wet,' moaned my mate, brushing the sweat out of her eyes. It was hard to stop it stinging as it mingled with suntan lotion, trickling down from under our hats.

We had started out thinking we looked cool in proper desert gear. Sarah was wearing a practical, legionnaire's style cap with a flap to cover the back of her neck.

I thought my cheap version of a Tilley hat, made of beige denim with a floppy brim, made me look like a proper explorer. Perhaps the string and toggle under my chin wasn't so cool but would keep it on in the wind. We felt, and must have looked, pretty silly; they were not our usual style.

'You know, short shorts are fine here in Mallorca, but I must buy some longer ones for our trip. I'd better get my pudgy knees covered up.'

'I don't know what you're worried about,' quipped Sarah.

'I don't want to offend anyone's sensibilities, although I don't think either of us rate as harem material these days,' I joked in reply.

'All I've got on is shorts, underwear and a t-shirt. It's little enough. Goodness knows what the Moroccans will think of us.

'I don't know how they get on with wearing so many clothes in the heat,' grumbled Sarah, looking and sounding hot and bothered.

'I've been reading online, and it seems as if the hotter it gets, the more they wrap up, long frocks and all.'

'Yes, I know, but then what about these packs on our backs? I know it's for our water supply, but two litres of water are quite heavy anyway, without all the other essential items we've been advised to take. It's all very well being told what we need to carry, but they don't bloomin' well have to carry it.'

'Take another slurp and lighten your load,' I nagged, watching her carefully.

Memories instantly popped into my mind of a once overheated Sarah fainting gently to the ground. As teenagers, we had a school outing to Wimbledon and had queued for hours to get into the Centre Court. A mere five minutes later, there she was, stretched out on the ground, overcome by the lack of air and high temperatures. No wonder I was a constant nag about drinking enough.

Dehydration is a real issue in the desert, and Charity Challenge had already sent us information updates, stressing the importance of carrying sufficient water. Two litres would only last for a morning whilst trekking in the dry heat of the Sahara.

We had agreed to watch out for one another, knowing we could spot signs of tiredness or distress that others might miss. The sense of mutual camaraderie was real, and a definite comfort in those wee small hours of the night when I was lying awake, curious but anxious about what we would face. Were we up to it? Our training wasn't going that smoothly.

'How are your knees?' asked my pal.

'Oh, OK, thanks,' I replied, trying to make light of the fact that we had both experienced aches and pains over the past few months. When Sarah had consulted her doctor about it, he laughed in complete disbelief at our plans.

'The Sahara Desert?' he chuckled. 'You've got fifty-year-old knees. I hope you have medical emergency insurance so you can pull out of this crazy trek?' he added, helpfully. My intrepid friend was incensed.

Telling me about this episode over the phone, she confessed his derogatory remarks had only made her more determined.

Yes, we did have fifty-year-old knees, but that didn't mean we were ready for the scrap heap just yet.

It would undoubtedly be a painful, tiring and demanding experience but telling us we were too old and worn out for it had the opposite effect. We were determined to show this sneering doctor he was wrong. Our knees would survive, we decided, popping the occasional painkiller when required.

'We'll show him,' we both heartily agreed.

It had seemed like a good idea for Sarah to come over to stay with us in Mallorca for a bit of a holiday plus a training week, also giving us time to exchange information and make some more of our interminable lists.

With only six weeks to go, we were well into preparations, trying out our kit and begging or borrowing all the items on our Charity Challenge packing list. They sent us frequent e-mails, directing and encouraging the training they thought we should be doing at this stage.

This particular September, it was still hot in Mallorca as we tried to acclimatise ourselves to the heat we would encounter in the desert. That explained why we walked in the middle of the day when most intelligent people were indoors, lying down in a cool and darkened room.

Boots had preoccupied us greatly. At only five feet tall, Sarah has tiny feet. Her expedition into Birmingham City Centre to visit outdoor pursuit shops had left her somewhat frustrated.

'Guess where I found my boots in the end?' she asked. 'You will never guess.'

'Go on then, tell me,' I prompted.

'In the children's section. They were half the price of adult boots and the only ones that would fit.' Being a tiny size three was paying unexpected dividends.

In a way, I think she was pleased as our costs were rapidly mounting, and footwear can come at quite a price.

I had decided to stick with my tried and tested leather boots, which I considered cooler than some modern synthetic fabrics. They were extremely comfortable and looked the part, being a tan colour and styled very much like traditional desert boots. I was relieved not to have to break in a new pair.

Over the past couple of months Sarah had done lots of walking and hers were well worn in.

Setting off this particular morning, we were very cheerful, although little worries niggled constantly. Would our knees hold up, would we cope with the weight of our daypacks, full of our daily needs, including those essential two litres of water? On the trek the rest of our camping paraphernalia would be carried in trucks, so we needed to be sure we had all the right things with us.

It helped to talk it through and compare notes. We had often chatted by Skype and e-mail in the months since deciding on our challenge, but it was so much easier in person.

Sarah had done a lot of hiking with a mate around the streets close to her home and some of the Welsh coastal path at weekends.

Initially, I felt a little intimidated by her efforts, but Mallorca was too hot throughout June, July and August. All I could manage was an hour or so, walking around the local lanes in the early morning or late evening.

I thought swimming every day would build up muscles and stamina, and that seemed like a far more pleasant method of training. I had planned to do more from September onwards, and this week was the start of my concerted campaign.

We began by walking along a little-used back road from Santa Maria, in the central plain of Mallorca, towards the Tramuntana Mountains. It meandered along between drystone walls and almond orchards, climbing as we headed towards Alaro, in the lee of the mountains.

It was our first time out together, and we wanted to check our relative speeds and let ourselves in gently. So, seven kilometres seemed like the right distance to be attempting.

'Hang on, let me get this set up.' Sarah had a programme on her I-phone to measure speed and distance, and it would be a useful tool in our training.

Trying to get into a rhythm, we were wending our way along this lane, past a few houses set in the countryside. Despite the insistent heat bouncing up from the roadway, there was plenty to attract our attention as we noticed plants sprawling over the walls, alongside colourful bougainvillea and vines weighed down with bunches of grapes.

The central plain of Mallorca is a prime wine-producing area, and the harvest was in full swing. The vine in my garden was laden down with bunches of ripe grapes, ready for me to pick and make my homebrew. The mere thought made us long for a cool drink to quench our increasing thirst.

Close to Alaro the drystone walls disappeared, and stunning vistas opened up. The Tramuntana Mountains are spectacular, and this village nestles at the foot of two enormous volcanic plugs on either side of a valley.

'Can you see the monastery?' I asked, pointing to the top of the nearest outcrop of rock. 'Just below it is a white building. That restaurant produces the best lamb I have ever tasted.' Sadly, it has been discovered by the celebrity chef brigade. When I first visited some twenty years ago, it still had outside toilets across the farmyard.

'Time for a celebratory shandy,' I suggested as we headed into the village, tired, grubby and hot, longing to sit down and rest.

Wending our way along the narrow, deserted streets, shutters were firmly closed against the heat of the day. The *pueblo* houses don't give much away. They are a blank canvas, their terracotta walls hiding the unseen depths of cool rooms with high, beamed ceilings, and concealed courtyards set around a well or an olive press.

Here is the real Mallorca, not the stuff of holiday brochures. There are still many traditions and a unique culture on the island if you take time to look for it.

We felt as if we were on an empty film set, waiting for the cool of the evening to come and the cast to appear and breathe life into it.

We plonked ourselves down on a couple of chairs. The dusty quiet of the central square was in complete contrast to the hustle and bustle of the market on Saturdays when families come out to bargain for fresh fruit and vegetables. Local people, both young and old, gather in the bars and cafes to exchange the time of day and quaff the local vino.

'Oh, it's good to put down this pack,' I exclaimed, slouching wearily onto the rather unwelcoming plastic chair.

Sarah got out her all-seeing, all-dancing phone to consult the oracle as we downed the welcome glasses of chilled shandy in double quick time, thirsty would-be trekkers that we were.

'How far have we walked? It felt like miles, and we've been going all morning. I'm so glad you move at the same pace as me,' I explained. 'Slowly, that is.'

There was little doubt that we would be bringing up the rear of any group, but we were somewhat concerned that we could be deemed too slow.

'Yes!' she exclaimed. 'Seven kilometres. That's good.' We had a congratulatory swig of our second drink and started doing our sums.

'That means we've been moving about two and a half kilometres an hour.' Instantly our upbeat mood switched to complete deflation.

That wasn't anywhere near good enough. We had enjoyed the hike but had spent all morning on this relatively short distance.

In a few brief weeks, we would experience temperatures above our current thirty degrees. We expected to walk about twenty-five kilometres a day for several days in a row with no break to recover our strength. With the need to take a rest in the shade during the searing midday heat, we would be hard-pressed to get into camp before dark, moving at our current pace. We were in trouble.

Sarah was suffering from the unaccustomed temperatures, red-faced and sweating, and we were both tramping along with fifty-year-old knees. What was to become of us?

'This is yummy,' I said, tucking into the delicious Mallorcan *Pepito de Lomo*, a baguette stuffed with salad and slices of pork loin fried in garlic and, on this occasion, some cheese melted over the whole lot. It was delicious, but pretty heavy and filling when there was the walk back to consider.

'You do realise we've still got seven kilometres to get home, and I feel stuffed?'

'Well, I am on holiday, and we are working up to our correct training level,' rationalised Sarah. 'Very, very slowly.'

We huffed and puffed our way wearily back along the narrow lanes in the lazy heat of that Indian summer afternoon.

We were enjoying the countryside, despite the increased effort needed to keep on going. We stopped several times to peer over drystone walls to watch farmers collecting ripe almonds from the trees. We were fascinated, watching their curious, dragon wing canvas contraptions catching the nuts as they were shaken vigorously from the trees.

'I think we should go to the beach tomorrow. We have got to try trekking in soft sand.'

'OK, Bossy One,' replied Sarah. I was Bossy One, for obvious reasons. My friend was Trod, which stands for Downtrodden One. It all goes back to our teenage years when I was full of "piss and vinegar", ready to take on the world. Sarah's approach was more measured both then and now. Her steely determination was to stand her in good stead during some challenging times.

That evening, as we chewed over the day's events, we realised the need to increase our speed if we were to keep up with everyone in November.

'Have you got the Charity Challenge checklist?' asked Sarah for the umpteenth time.

Having prepared separately, albeit through frequent e-mails, we were making full use of our week together to ensure we were ready. We had been surprised to learn we needed three-season sleeping bags which would have sufficient insulation to keep us warm in the chilly desert nights. Plus, lotions, potions and the general detritus of camping, including possibly a mallet to assist in erecting our tents every night.

Yes, we were to camp in the vast desert, amongst the dunes, under the canopy of stars, an enticing if somewhat scary prospect. We were trying to focus on the positives as opposed to the possible negatives, like humongous spiders and ferocious scorpions sharing our space.

I was grateful that we would only have to carry our daypacks with essentials for a full day hike. My shoulders are no longer up to lugging around heavy camping equipment. A desert trek, yes, but I do know my limitations.

That was part of the reason we had used an established company that organises these challenges regularly. Neither we nor our respective charities were up to arranging an independent trip. We would be joining a group on a pre-arranged route with full local support in the form of guides, cooks and porters. Luxury trekking? If you think so, you get out there and try it!

The following morning, we gathered our gear together and headed up to the north of Mallorca to the slightly more rustic beaches of Muro. They are not as manicured as the ones in the south, and we hoped we wouldn't stand out quite so much amongst the holidaymakers.

'Oh blast, I've got sand in my boots. We'll have to stop again.'

'Me too,' groaned Sarah. Long trousers might have been a better option for our beach training to help keep it out. So that was why gaiters were on our kit list. I had wondered.

In thirty-five degrees (almost one hundred degrees in old money), on a nudist beach with sunbathers spread all around on colourful towels and sun loungers, we didn't want to make a spectacle of ourselves. However, we did attract some curious looks.

'I feel ridiculous,' my pal moaned.

'Really?' I replied through gritted teeth.

Picture this: shorts, charity t-shirts, hiking boots, daypacks and water bottles plus our daft hats. Did we look out of place on a nudist beach? We certainly did.

The all-seeing, all-dancing phone announced that we had walked a paltry two kilometres in an hour. Even allowing for the loose sand we had been trudging through, it wasn't enough, and we were shattered.

This sand is heavy going.

Was it a desert mirage before us? No, a *chiringuito* (a Spanish bar/restaurant, thoughtfully located right on the beach).

'We're having an "away day" cos I am on my hols you know,' justified Sarah as our mouth-watering lunch of locally caught fresh fish arrived.

'OK, but we'll have to do some proper training tomorrow,' I nagged, before tucking into our feast with gusto.

We have GOT to get serious about this trekking lark.

By the time Sarah left Mallorca, we had managed a long walk, inland from the south coast towards Calvia. We seemed to be out all day, but only covered about eighteen kilometres, some of it gently uphill. We were still slow but starting to feel encouraged by our improved walking speed and more ease of movement.

We had managed to bolster one another's confidence and were looking forward to our trek. We felt better prepared and ready to face the challenge, and we still had a further six weeks to train on our own. Mentally we were on top form.

CHAPTER FIVE
Disaster Strikes

'Do you realise you've only got four weeks left for training?' asked Bernie, poking his head out from under the car.

'Yeah, yeah. Are you trying to scare me?' I jokily replied, bending down again to the ever-present task of weeding our jungle of a garden.

Now he had reminded me, and I began to work it out. I was well aware of how time was flying while we were so busy in our daily lives, but his comment focused my mind.

'Blimey, you're right. There is less than a month left and still so much to do. Will you time me this afternoon while I walk around the block?' I asked, knowing that Bernie was keen to get me moving faster than my usual amble. We were hoping to get me around a five-kilometre loop in under an hour.

Supportive as ever, he was an integral part of this effort, and I felt secure in the knowledge that he was right alongside me, figuratively when not in person.

'Slowcoach. I'll get next door's dog to chase you if you're not careful,' he joked, coming over to give me a quick kiss. 'I'll make a cuppa,' he yelled over his shoulder as he headed indoors.

I sighed, thinking how lucky I was to have such a lovely guy in my life and bent down again to concentrate on the weeds.

'Tea's ready, come and get it.'

'On my way,' I yelled as I started to straighten up. That's when everything changed, and the challenge began.

'Ow!' I shouted, stopping abruptly, still partially bent over in agony, afraid to move.

'What's the matter?' called Bernie from the terrace.

'That bloody hurt!' I shouted, holding one hand against my back which had gone into spasm, sending pain like a bolt of electricity through my body.

Straightening slowly and carefully, moaning and groaning, I wasn't even fully upright before I started moving slowly towards the house. I looked and felt like a little old lady, crouched over, hobbling along.

'Oh no, not now,' I thought. 'Not my back.' I stopped, sweat trickling between my shoulder blades, as I stood still to let things ease up. With only four weeks to go, this was all I needed. Panicked thoughts whirled around my brain.

'Come and lie down on the sofa. I'm sure it's just a tweak. Why don't you take the day off and rest it?' Bernie sounded calm and reassuring as I manoeuvred myself carefully and painfully down into the squishy nest of cushions I had bounced out of last night, full of "vim and vigour", a far cry from the sorry sight I was now.

'OK, OK, don't boss me about,' I replied, the pain adding a sharp edge to my tongue. 'I've got lots to be getting on with, I suppose. There are loads of lists to write and e-mails to keep me busy for the moment.' I settled in for a quiet couple of days, hoping that would solve the problem.

A short time later, I threw my well-thumbed guidebook to Morocco onto the floor and huffed in exasperation. I'm not known for my patience. I had been enjoying my daily training, pounding the lanes surrounding our home, pushing myself to move faster and with more ease. I was also into my dance training for the "Not So Strictly!" competition, challenging myself to learn both the waltz and cha-cha-cha, stretching muscles I had forgotten I had. Back problems were the last thing I needed. I never dreamt it would get so bad that I couldn't even walk.

A couple of days later, Bernie was getting impatient.

'Are you feeling any better?' he asked, for the umpteenth time, approaching me, carefully judging my mood.

I was in a funk, and anything could make me snap, concerned as I was about the pain I was in, the trek, organising, training, you name it. Yet, here I was, confined to the sofa, worrying about it.

'You've been stretched out there, fretting yourself into a frenzy.'

'Yes, I know,' my voice trembling as I fought to keep the ever-present tears at bay.

'Come on, love, you're like a leaky tap. Get up and show me where it hurts,' he urged. 'You can't carry on like this, and I hate to see you in such a state. Walk around a bit so I can see what's going on.'

Pulling myself carefully upright, spasms of pain shot spitefully across my back as I tried not to grimace and make more of things than perhaps they actually were.

'Oof,' I groaned, sharp slivers of agony running like lightning down into my left thigh, making it impossible to put my foot on the floor.

'Why are you standing like that? You look like an injured horse.' An apt description and, although I tried not to wince, Bernie could see quite clearly how difficult it was for me to shuffle even a few steps.

Watching his face, I lowered myself wearily back onto the sofa, dreading his reaction. Lying around had given me ample time to fret myself into a dark place, fearful that all my plans were in ruins.

His impatience was nothing compared to how I was feeling. I was itching to get back to training, both walking and dancing.

'Try these, love. You've taken them before, so we know they work.'

Swallowing a cocktail of painkillers and anti-inflammatories, I could feel my stomach contract in rebellion. What was I doing to myself? Was it worth all this angst?

'Do you think the pills are helping at all?' asked Bernie later that evening as he nuked us a curry straight from the freezer.

I leant against the kitchen counter, trying not to flinch.

'I don't think so,' I conceded.

Lying awake in the wee small hours of the night, I tried not to keep him awake with my laboured tossing and turning. My resolve was starting to weaken when he finally brought things to a head.

'Do you think it's time to get a bit of help?' he suggested gently, watching my face for my reaction. 'So that at least we know what's going on. What about a physiotherapist?'

'Mmm, maybe,' I said, aware that was an admission in itself, but this problem wasn't going to go away, and I was worrying at it like a dog with a bone and getting nowhere.

'We've tried self-help, and it isn't working,' Bernie insisted, gently gauging my mood.

'Am I being a drama queen?'

'No, I can see you're in pain. I think a professional opinion would be helpful.'

I felt better in myself once we had a plan and got to work phoning around for an appointment at short notice.

We both knew Tracey Evans from her years working with yacht crews, and I was lucky that she agreed to squeeze me into her busy schedule.

The following morning, I couldn't put my left foot on the ground without setting off searing pain in my leg. My back no longer seemed to be the issue. What was going on?

'Can you drop me right outside the office? I can't walk very far,' I nagged. Bernie sensibly kept quiet and parked right by the door.

Hobbling inside, I was shown straight to the therapy room, obviously in too much of a state to sit in the waiting area. I could smell liniment in the air and hoped that would be the solution.

My heart was in my mouth, dreading the possible outcome of this appointment. Finally recognising I needed help to solve this problem had been a big admission for me to make.

'Can you get yourself up on the couch?' Tracey asked, gently offering me her shoulder to lean on as I tried carefully to hoist myself up.

Completely overwrought, shaking from the pain shooting from my back and down into my left thigh, I struggled to lie down. Straightening my legs was agony. I felt like curling up into a ball to relieve things, hoping it would all go away.

I will admit to being a bit of a wuss at times and was wary of making a mountain out of this particular molehill, but I had never experienced anything like it before. No doubt it doesn't compare to childbirth, but it was taxing me to my limits.

As Tracey gently massaged my thigh, I yelled out loud with tears streaming down my face. My left leg twitched and jerked under her gentle hands; all illusion of self-control had vanished into thin air.

'I'm sorry to be such a baby,' I gasped, even now aware that I could be overreacting.

Her reassurance that I was no worse than any other client calmed me down a little bit, and I tried to start an intelligent conversation about my situation, but Tracey had other ideas.

'Just rest now, Dawne,' she threw over her shoulder as she left the room, leaving me distraught, frightened, and feeling properly sorry for myself.

If you have ever had sciatic pain, you will have some sympathy for my predicament, but the problem was in the front of my thigh.

Overhearing voices, I realised Tracey was talking to Bernie.

'When exactly does Dawne plan to leave?' I heard her say, followed by a muffled reply.

The tension in the room was palpable as she came back to me. Not allowing her to speak, I began to tell her about my schedule, gabbling my words in the vain hope that spelling it out would get me a fast-tracked cure. I was eager to resume training again.

'I'm due to leave in less than four weeks. That's why I'm so uptight about it all,' I confessed, as the tears came again. 'This trek is so important to me, and everyone has been very generous. I can't let them down,' I explained, going on to tell her about the upcoming dance competition too, even promising a poster for her to put up in the clinic.

Determined to carry on as planned, I would not countenance any changes. If it was possible to will yourself better, it would have worked for me.

'Let's leave things to settle down over the weekend. Come in on Monday, and we'll do some more work to ease the inflammation in your back. I think that's causing the femoral nerve running down the front of your thigh to go into spasm, and that's what is causing this pain,' she explained.

She made it sound like something we could make progress with, but would things happen quickly enough for me?

As I hobbled out of the clinic, and carefully climbed into the car, my mind was buzzing with possibilities. Perhaps it would all be over by Monday? I was kidding myself, of course, but I needed some hope to grasp onto.

'Can I get you anything?' asked Bernie later on, solicitous as ever. 'If not, I'm going back to the garage,' he added, knowing that sympathy would only make me lash out at him.

'No, thanks. Sorry I'm miserable,' I added. 'I'm so worried about the trek.'

I settled back on the sofa, my brain aching from constantly working through the possible ways of dealing with the situation.

We had talked in the car about the various treatments available, how long I would have to wait for an improvement and what it meant for my training. We both felt a little more upbeat, having grasped the nettle and started to face up to things.

My mind was in turmoil after another sleepless night. I was unable to lie in comfort or do anything without pain.

I had taken the occasional painkiller but was reluctant to mask things as I wanted to know if it was easing off. No such luck. If anything, it was worse.

I couldn't walk more than a few paces without experiencing shooting pains in my left leg, and my thigh was now completely numb when I poked or prodded it. The only sensation was a tingling deep inside the muscle, a new and worrying development.

Discussing this over breakfast, Bernie was in no mood to let things lie for the weekend.

'Let's get off to the hospital now,' he suggested, having pressed firmly into my thigh and got no response from me.

'Even my skin has changed. Look, it's flabby and kind of doughy, like uncooked bread.' There was little resistance, even from the healthy muscle mass I had built up in training.

'I don't think we should wait until Monday. You're even worse than you were yesterday. If they can organise some x-rays, then at least we'll be able to see exactly what's going on.'

I have to admit I was relieved at this suggestion. We all hate hospitals, but at this point I was willing to try anything that might sort out things out.

I was a sorry sight as we pulled up outside the Accident and Emergency department, hobbling along and bent almost double, a far cry from the bouncy, fit and enthusiastic person you would have met a few days previously.

The ladies who work at our local clinic are absolute stars. They work as translators and all-round organisers for the Brits who need hospital treatment, and they have never failed to help me out in times of ill health. Sadly, they know me only too well.

'Hi, Dawne, how are you?' asked Vivienne. I have always thought that is a daft question to ask in a hospital.

'Not very well,' I replied, mistress of the understatement, swaying on my feet and grimacing in pain.

'Sit down and tell me the problem,' she invited, and we began our explanations.

Getting straight on the phone, Viv worked her magic. Asking the occasional question and seeming to understand my concern about time running out, she got me in to see a specialist that same day.

'You can also have an MRI scan first thing on Sunday morning if you can make it?'

'Really? That's fantastic,' I replied, surprised, but it was still tourist season, and the clinics stayed open all available hours to cope with the constant stream of sick and injured visitors.

It was a relief to know we would have a picture of what was happening in my back so quickly, although it would take a week to get the results.

Bernie and I amused ourselves with people-watching while waiting around to see doctors. However, being a hospital, all too often their stories were ones of sadness, if not tragedy. Pain all around us, he resorted to telling me jokes and reading daft things from the internet to keep me from sinking into despair.

Once we got in front of the specialist, Bernie's terrier-like qualities came to the fore, worrying at the problem and looking for solutions, not letting go, like a dog with a bone. I was lucky to have him with me as the whole appointment passed in a blur. Tired and distressed, my Spanish deserted me. Our trusty translator was a godsend.

After some prodding and poking, the doctor suspected that I had compressed a disc in my lower back, and the MRI scan would confirm his diagnosis that it was resting on the femoral nerve, resulting in all the pain. His conclusion was that time to heal was the primary factor, and that was just what I didn't have.

'But how much time?' I wailed. Cue that typical Spanish shrug, *no lo se*, I don't know.

Pills were rattling in my pocket as I hopped gingerly into the house and back onto the sofa. They were mainly painkillers and anti-inflammatories which, because of my clotting condition, had to be given the OK for me to take. Our lovely ladies in Customer Services had telephoned my haematologist (at his home, I might add) to check they were safe.

Factor V Leiden affects everything I do, not least when prescribed any drug. For example, I had not realised that antimalarials can affect the viscosity of the blood and that the only one safe for me to take is Malarone. Having taken all of the other available options at some time in my life, I can only think that I have had a lucky escape.

By nine o'clock that night, we were both worn out.

'Let's have a glass of wine,' I suggested wearily. Bernie had shown admirable patience and kindness, enduring the interminable hanging around, sitting with me in the hospital café, staying positive in the face of my overwhelming negativity.

I just couldn't believe that I could get any answers and felt fearful of those I might get. He stayed upbeat, sure there was a magic solution at hand.

****

'Can you make it to the car without me?' asked Bernie. We were about to leave on our daily run to the hospital for an injection into the muscles of my lower back.

Added to the load of pills I had to take while waiting for the MRI scan result, this problem had taken over our lives.

At least the specialist had seemed relatively unconcerned about my symptoms. He had listened carefully to my worries about being ready for the trek in just under four weeks. This was about to be the longest month of my life.

The injections helped to numb the pain in my back but were only a short-term fix.

A week later, he could see exactly what was going on. He seemed quite cheerful, explaining that the inflamed disc in my back was resting against the femoral nerve, which extends down into the thigh, and that was the reason why my leg wasn't working properly. Only time would allow that swelling to subside and the pain to ease.

It was hardly life-threatening and, under normal circumstances, I would have "put up and shut up", but time was of the essence....

****

A couple of days later, I reluctantly picked up the phone.

'Ian, I'm sorry but I simply can't do the "Not So Strictly!" dance competition anytime soon. I have a serious back problem, and I'm in too much pain to train.' My hand was shaking as I blurted this admission before I had time to back out.

I hate letting people down, and this wasn't just about the dancing. I hadn't anticipated such generosity from local businesses and all those lovely people who had donated raffle prizes. Not fulfilling my part of the bargain made me feel wretched. It was a dismal situation,

79

and I felt that I was also failing in my obligation to Thrombosis UK.

Bernie and I discussed it endlessly, testing his patience. Whilst he understood my concerns, I did chew over and over the problem; the rights, wrongs and practicalities of putting off this event.

The sad fact was that I simply couldn't train, or dance or, for that matter, sit, stand or even walk properly. The pain was constant and overwhelming. I couldn't control the sharp stabbing into my thigh, which was still numb to the touch, like uncooked dough.

'Well, as you're not fit, I think we will have to postpone it. Don't worry too much, injuries are common,' Ian replied. That was easy for him to say.

He was quite matter of fact which made me feel a little better about the situation, and we hadn't yet done a proper blitz of advertising.

However, I was dreading contacting everyone who had offered raffle prizes. They had all come up trumps with offers of a spa day in a five-star hotel, tickets to the top international show on the island, handmade jewellery and many more besides.

Reluctantly we agreed the dancing had to go on hold.

'I'll draft a letter to my sponsors, Ian, but I will mention the dance school and your commitment to running the event sometime after my return. Is that OK?'

'Of course it is,' he replied. 'Take it easy and let me know how you're getting on. We're all wishing you lots of luck.'

I sent out e-mails explaining I was injured, making it clear my main concern was the trek. So, the dance competition would be rescheduled for a later date. I wasn't about to admit there was any doubt about me getting to Morocco.

The many kind and concerned replies I received improved my mood, as everyone promised to provide the offered prizes at a future date. At least I could relax about that.

However, with only two weeks before I was due to leave, the situation was pretty dire.

'How far did you get?' asked Bernie, determinedly upbeat as I limped through our garden gates one sunny evening.

'Only down to the railway line,' I wailed.

It's about a hundred metres from our house, and it had been an agonising walk.

I was still unable to put my left foot firmly to the ground, without that all-consuming pain shooting down the femoral nerve into my thigh, which stubbornly remained numb to the touch. Improvement was very, very slow.

'Shall I come with you tomorrow?' offered Bernie, determined to keep me focused on the positives. 'We'll try and get around the block together, even if you have to stop and rest several times.'

'That would be great. At least I'll have you to lean on,' I muttered, grateful for his support but seriously doubting it would be possible.

The following day, we set off. Every few steps I had to stop and lift my leg, whilst attempting to hold my breath. It was the only way to minimise the agonising darts of nerve pain that I couldn't control. I have never experienced anything like it.

I had always thought the stabbing sensation and breathing difficulties caused by the blood clot in my lung so many years ago would top the list of painful episodes in my life, but this was something else.

Returning to my accustomed perch on the sofa, I was trying to carry on as usual, but it was difficult. I was avoiding driving, and I was lucky enough to have Bernie as my willing chauffeur.

Everywhere I went, I was trying to cover up the problem, as I didn't want to let people know how bad I felt or that there was even a remote chance I might not be able to go on the trek.

Joining friends one night for dinner, they explained away my hobbling gait by assuming I had blisters from training. If only. Choosing not to enlighten them and wanting to avoid their sympathy, I kept my fears to myself.

'Do you think it's time to talk to Sarah?' I asked Bernie, as I had most evenings. She had no idea of the severity of the pain I was in, or that I had difficulty walking.

'Is it fair to tell her?' he replied. 'She'll only worry.'

'You may be right. She's concerned enough about the actual trek as it is. Morocco can be quite a shock to the system if you've never been out of Europe before, and I know she's worried about coping with the physical demands too.'

'Yes, I realise that. Perhaps it's best to keep it to ourselves until the last minute. There's nothing she can do to help anyway.'

What we were forgetting was the old saying that "a problem shared is a problem halved". In hindsight, I can see it was a mistake. Sarah worried that she had not heard from me. I realise it was a selfish decision, but, at the time, it seemed better to keep the problem to myself.

I hadn't told Charity Challenge either, as I was sure they would want to move me to a later trip if I was physically unfit. However, I wasn't confident that they would move Sarah with me as there was nothing wrong with her. It was vital to me that we did this together for many reasons. I had got her into this and felt honour bound to be alongside her. It would have been awful, in my mind, for us to take part separately, as it was our joint adventure.

I didn't realise that my friend was getting more and more concerned as time went on. She was worried sick, and Bernie was just plain old sick of me and my constant running over the same ground. I was messing things up big time.

He was very gung ho about things, steadfastly refusing to believe that I could not complete the trek, and he wanted it over and done with because it was taking over our lives.

Looking back, I realise that challenges of this nature require physical fitness, and that injuries are common. Some manage to achieve their goals, while others have to postpone, but the general public seem to be very sympathetic with such things. It might have been better to let everyone know by putting updates on my Just Giving fundraising page as I went along. A different approach and perhaps a more balanced one, but I couldn't see beyond my situation and the dread of letting everyone down.

I eventually confided in a close friend who was so encouraging.

'I don't care whether or not you complete this. You've done so much with your fundraising efforts, and your intentions are clear. The money is for Thrombosis UK, and everyone has donated to them in support of you. That belief in you is there whether or not you do the trek.' Bless her. She made me feel quite humbled.

Each day Bernie and I managed a few steps further. We came back from a brief shopping trip with a sports style back brace, which I began to try out.

'Has it made any difference do you think?' he asked, on my return from a laboured walk around a very short block.

'Actually, yes,' I admitted, a rare shaft of optimism emerging from the gloom. 'I'll use it every day as it keeps me in a more upright position, but I don't know if I can manage a daypack,' I fretted.

'I've just dug out an old one which seems smaller and lighter than yours,' he replied. 'Try that out tomorrow, even if you carry nothing but a litre of water to see how it feels.'

A week before my departure, I was pushing myself further every day. We even resurrected an old pair of hiking poles to give me something to lean on or push against whilst attempting to train.

Just five days before leaving, I had jubilantly managed to hike the seven kilometres to Alaro. It had been a slow and painful process, with sweat dripping down my body and soaking the back brace. It was a far cry from the happy journey I had enjoyed with Sarah so recently, but I was pleased, although still nagging Bernie daily with my worries.

It was a long way short of the distance I would have to walk each day, often through soft and uneven, shifting sand. Was this a challenge too far?

'OK. We have to make a final decision today. Do I go for it?'

'I think you should,' replied Bernie, steadfast as ever. There were only four days before I was due to leave, and we still had to get an agreement from the doctors. Was it even worth seeing them?

'Let's go and see what they have to say. If you can get away without causing further injury, then I still think you can do it,' he insisted.

'I really, really want to go,' I whispered tentatively, afraid to admit it.

The appointment at the hospital was crucial. If the doctor said no, that would be the end of it. We had left things as late as possible, but ignoring medical opinion wasn't an option.

My heart was pounding with nerves as I walked carefully into the specialist's office with confidence I didn't feel, head held high and holding my breath.

Sitting down in front of two doctors, I realised with relief that they knew exactly why I was there. I had taken the precaution of getting Vivienne to talk with them before our meeting, so they appreciated the importance of what they were about to say. They were both smiling, which gave me a boost. Either it was good news, or they thought I was mad.

'How is it, this pain?' the older doctor asked.

'OK, OK,' I lied, feeling sweat run down my back. 'I'm due to leave in four days. Am I fit to go?' I asked, on the verge of tears as I sucked in my breath, waiting for his reply.

Totally focused on them as they nodded cautiously to one another, I was oblivious to the usual antiseptic smells of hospital consulting rooms and the echoing clatter of other patients in the hallway outside.

'You will be in more pain as the trek progresses, and you ask more of your body,' the younger of the two explained. His English was quite good, and he seemed to understand what this was all about. My heart sank. 'It will slow down your recovery but go prepared, and you will be fine. You cannot cause more damage, just extra pain from the inflammation.'

They prescribed more of the strong pain relievers which could be injected straight into the muscles of my lower back. Explaining that we had a medic on our trip, it would be possible to administer these in case of emergency, and I reassured them that provision had been made for me to leave if needs be.

That was just Bernie ensuring I had enough money to get to a hotel and contact him should I have to pull out. At least I could speak some French. I could communicate with the non-Arabic speaking Moroccans should the situation arise.

Elated at the outcome of the hospital visit, we left wreathed in smiles. I was grateful for the input of all the Customer Services team who had pushed so hard to get me early appointments and scans and keeping my hopes alive. With their shouts of 'Good luck!' ringing in my ears, we hugged Vivienne and headed home.

'Yes! I'm on it,' I enthused to Bernie, who was keeping any reservations well hidden. 'We deserve a drink to celebrate!' I yelled. 'I *will* be on this trek.' In high spirits, we drove back home to concentrate on my packing.

Those four days were still fraught with doubts. Rather than push my body, we decided I should rest for the time remaining. It would give my back, leg and thigh the best chance to heal as much as possible before I really had to exert them. My overall fitness level was high, despite having lost some muscle mass over those four painful weeks.

We were sure the challenge was within my capabilities if all things were equal. It was simply a matter of coping with the pain.

Above all, I was fired up with enthusiasm and determination. Each time I wavered, there was Bernie, bolstering my resolve. There is one thing for sure, without his endless reserves of patience and optimism, it would have been a very different story.

Ringing Sarah that evening, I mentioned little of this battle.

'You will be there, won't you?' She sounded nervous and lacking in confidence.

'Of course I will. I'll be somewhere in the depths of Casablanca Airport, in the domestic terminal. I have a bit of a wait before you are due to arrive. It will be so good to see you.'

I would be there, but in what state I couldn't say.

'This is it! It's going to be great. Don't worry about anything, we'll be fine,' I reassured her.

'OK, Bossy One. See you on Saturday.' Sarah sounded wary but eager to get on with our adventure. I was as ready as I ever would be. Or was I?

****

In an attempt to keep life jogging along as normal, despite everything, I was at the Lions Club charity shop bright and early on Friday morning for my usual weekly shift as a volunteer, along with Hazel and our Scottish friend Sandy.

'Here, use my keys,' I insisted as Hazel struggled to get her own set to work in the temperamental locks of the shutters.

We were eager to open up and greet the hordes of people we were sure would soon arrive to inspect our wares. "In your dreams", to coin a phrase.

As it was November, Palma Nova was deserted. Most tourists had left us to our winter peace and quiet. Situated in the heart of the English resorts in the south of Mallorca it was, of course, quite another story in the holiday season.

We weren't anticipating a busy morning, but we began to set up the shop, pulling rails of clothes outside onto the terrace, along with baskets of shoes and toys. While waiting for our first customer, we were soon gossiping over a cup of tea.

'Are you organised, Dawne?' asked Hazel. 'Time has flown by so quickly. I can't believe you're leaving in the morning,' she added. 'It's so exciting.'

'Well, I'm kind of disorganised,' I confessed.

I hadn't told the girls the full extent of my fears. They had drawn their own conclusions about the pain I was in, but I was doggedly determined to keep my concerns to myself and had generally blustered about how well things were going. Disorganisation was not my usual problem and this confession, in itself, told a story.

At that time, there were some concessions available. One of them was half price travel to the mainland. My flight to Morocco started from Madrid, so I had a special fare booked from Palma.

However, the rules had changed (yet again) on what paperwork was necessary to prove eligibility for that rate.

'Do either of you know what documents are needed now?' I asked, with some trepidation, having spent time the previous day getting a variety of answers.

I hadn't focused on such details until I was sure I was going on the trip, hence the last-minute panic on this one. The day before, I had managed to convince myself I had the correct papers but couldn't resist another check.

'I've just booked for Barcelona,' said Sandy. 'I had to go to the town hall to get the new permission form. You can't travel without it,' she stated firmly.

It was the opposite of all I had been told, and I suddenly realised that I could be prevented from travel on the big day without the correct paperwork.

'Damn, it was a fiesta in our village yesterday, so that was the one office I couldn't consult.' Panic was starting to set in again. This was just what I didn't need at this late stage. More fool me for not checking earlier.

A flurry of phone calls later, it was clear I needed another form, and the town hall was closing early, at half past twelve, as part of the ongoing fiesta.

'It's already eleven o'clock, and I don't have my car. Damn, damn, damn.' My voice quivered as tears threatened.

Up until now, my weak moments had been for Bernie's eyes only, but this setback loomed large in my overstressed brain. Bluster had always been my fall-back position, never letting anyone know the extent of my problems and fears. However, there's always the straw that breaks the camel's back.

Sandy, with her no-nonsense approach, came to my rescue.

'So, are you saying that you need to get to the town hall in the next hour, and you don't have a car to get there?' she asked. I felt like one of her school pupils, confessing that the dog had eaten my homework.

Our village is a half-hour drive from the shop, and I would need to go home to pick up my passport. However you looked at it, time was of the essence, and, at this point, I was considering taxis and trains; anything to get me there in time.

'Take mine. Here are the keys,' Sandy said, making light of it. 'Look for a silver Clio with a big dent down the driver's side door. You can't miss it in the car park.'

I huffed and puffed for a moment before gratefully accepting her generous and unexpected offer, and away I went, hurrying as fast as my back would allow. It was a good job I was on my made-up regime of painkillers.

Driving carefully home, I berated myself for being stupid enough to leave something so important until the very last minute. Reciting yoga chants over and over in my head, wanting the universe to be on my side, I pulled into our driveway to grab my passport. Willing the town hall to be open, I needed the formalities to be straightforward and get things sorted without delay.

It was my own fault. Spanish paperwork is notoriously complex, and government organisations have a reputation for being difficult, but my luck held.

The lady in the office was keen to get away for the fiesta celebrations, so it took her less than half an hour to organise, and, by half past twelve, I was back in the charity shop, regaling my friends with the details.

'Well, that's a relief,' said Sandy.

'You can say that again. I can't thank you enough for the use of your car,' I cheerfully replied. 'Can you think of anything else I might have forgotten?' I was determined not to get caught out by anything else my addled brain may have overlooked.

'Oh, I think you're good to go,' reassured Hazel.

By then, I was on a high, lifted by their positivity and belief in me. Thanks, girls. Without your support through this challenge, it would have been so much harder to achieve.

When I left the shop, I was ready to slay dragons. Nothing was going to stop me now.

CHAPTER SIX
Day One – Morocco Bound

I was finally on my way. In a few short hours, I would be on the plane, but finding motivation was like catching hold of a slippery eel, constantly eluding my grasp.

Taking a few minutes to mentally prepare, I wondered what the next week would bring; would I cope, or would I be sending an urgent message to Bernie to come and get me out of trouble?

'Did you sleep well?' he asked, hopeful as ever that I would be in a positive frame of mind.

'Not really,' I replied, already feeling bone-weary.

'Never mind. I'll get breakfast ready while you get dressed.' He wandered off to the kitchen, leaving me to try and buck myself up.

'Come on, Trekker Girl,' I muttered. 'This is no time for doubts. Get a grip.'

Despite edging slowly out of bed, stabbing pains shot down my left leg. Holding my breath, I pulled on my cotton trousers and charity t-shirt, ready to face the world.

'Tea or coffee?' asked Bernie, sticking his head around the bedroom door.

'Tea, please, and I'll take a couple of painkillers at the same time,' I replied, trying to sound upbeat while ignoring the weird sensations in my thigh. It was so strange how it tingled inside but felt numb to the touch.

By moving carefully, I minimised the chance of jarring my leg or back. However, there was some challenging trekking coming up.

Feeling the nervous churning in my stomach, I forced myself to eat a good breakfast to ensure it was well lined to deal with the procession of pills I was relying on to get me through the day.

'You look like a proper trekker,' Bernie said affectionately. 'You're all set to go, I'm so proud of you. Look at the camera, I want to get the "before" photo.'

I'm on my way.

'Goodness knows what state I'll be in when I get back,' I replied, staring around and fidgeting with my bags.

'Are you ready?' Bernie asked, taking pictures of me with my daypack on, ready to conquer all.

I felt comfortable in the overcast weather that morning, despite the unaccustomed tightness of the back brace wrapped around my body. Having used it over the past few days, I felt it was worth a try, but I was going to be sweaty, for sure.

Fashioned out of lightweight breathable materials and padded with plastic supports, it covered me from the base of my spine to midriff, lying flat against my skin, underneath my t-shirt and trousers so no one would notice it.

My phone was constantly beeping with messages of encouragement, and I was still feeling the warmth from Bernie's heartfelt hugs as I slowly walked into the airport terminal in Palma.

The whole place was a hive of activity with hordes of travellers, laden with luggage, bustling from check-in to security, busy as ants collecting crumbs. Yet, I had never felt so alone in my life.

How ridiculous. I was wallowing in self-pity and fretting about the challenge ahead. There was so much to look forward to. Why was I still worrying about whether or not I was plain arrogant and idiotic to think I could take this on with my back in such a state?

I took some reassurance from the words of the doctors, which rang in my ears.

'Don't be afraid of the pain. It will get worse, but you will not damage yourself further. You are asking your body to do far more than it should at this point in your recovery, and it will complain, but embrace it. You know what is causing it.'

I had injections to be administered in case of emergency and enough money to get myself home should I have to abandon the trek. As long as I could get to a town, I could manage. Knowing how efficient Charity Challenge had been so far, I was sure they had the resources on the ground to get me to civilisation fairly quickly if needs be.

With this in mind, I gave myself a good talking to and not before time.

'Behave yourself, girl. This is no time for self-pity; you've done it. You're ready to go, and this is the adventure of a lifetime. It hasn't been an easy run-up, but this is it! Get on with it and enjoy the experience.'

I should also have been thinking of Sarah. Never having been outside of Europe before, she would find some aspects of this trip worrying. I had to pay attention to her needs too. Above all, this was supposed to be fun.

My thoughts whirled around as I felt the weight of responsibility on my shoulders. I was thinking of my friend and the many people who had donated to Thrombosis UK. They were all relying on the strength of my commitment to do this.

While the rest of our group were flying from Heathrow, I was flying from Mallorca via Madrid. I had elected to join them in Casablanca where we were due to take a short flight across to Ouarzazate in eastern Morocco, the jumping-off point for our trek.

Just the mention of Casablanca conjured up all sorts of romantic images in my mind (Humphrey Bogart uppermost I have to admit), and I was looking forward to seeing it for myself.

The short flight to Madrid takes about fifty minutes. However, it only takes ninety minutes to lose 50% of the blood flow in our legs which puts everyone at risk of thrombosis. With that in mind, I disturbed my neighbour during the flight so that I could get up and move about – better safe than sorry.

'Excuse me, please,' I said. '*Por favor*,' I tried, not knowing where he was from.

'Sorry,' came the reply in English.

The man was wearing a formal business suit which was quite at odds with my somewhat scruffy appearance. I already looked creased and crumpled.

As I squeezed back into my seat, I bent forwards to adjust my socks.

'Those look uncomfortable,' he observed.

'Oh, they are. They're not exactly elegant either,' I replied.

'Aren't they a bit warm for this weather?'

'Well, yes.'

'So why are you wearing them?' he asked curiously.

'It's a case of having to really,' I began, not sure how much he would want to hear.

'I had two blood clots when I was only twenty-six. These are called compression socks and are supposed to help prevent another one,' I explained.

They come up to my knees and are made of elastic, fitting snugly but not tightly. Unpleasant to wear at the best of times, they are horrible in the heat. But there it is. As far as I am concerned, they are essential on any flight to help guard against the formation of a Deep Vein Thrombosis. (See my note in the introduction)

Sitting back, I mulled over what I had told him. Did he want to know more?

'That sounds pretty serious.'

'You're quite right, it is. Flying is always a risk for me, so I take extra care. I also take a 75mg aspirin for a couple of days before a flight,' I added. 'It's not a remedy aimed directly at Factor Five Leiden sufferers; it is a precautionary measure that anyone can take to thin the blood. I am just super careful.'

'What's the Factor Five thing?' he queried, looking interested.

That was my opening. The rest of the flight passed in the blink of an eye. I told him about this clotting disorder, and how there are many preventative measures I can take. Drinking water is essential for everyone, to counteract dehydration when flying. I even avoid caffeine and alcohol for the twenty-four hours before and during travel. Both of these constrict blood vessels.

'I hadn't realised that blood clots were so much of a risk,' he said. 'I just think of old people getting them, yet you had yours when you were quite young. Thank you,' he said. 'You've taught me a few things I won't forget. Good luck with everything. You look dressed for adventure,' were his final words. I hadn't even had time to tell him where I was off to.

On arrival at Madrid, I collected my scruffy wheelie bag, which I had chosen as there was absolutely no way I could have manhandled my luggage or carried a heavy backpack. We had a fifteen-kilo weight restriction imposed by the ground crew in Morocco as they would be lugging our gear twice a day between the top of their trucks and our tents. At least they weren't using traditional desert transport; wheelie bags aren't flexible enough for a camel's back.

Madrid is an international airport with several terminals, and Air Maroc were based in one a long way from my arrival point. It could take as long as an hour to move between them.

I had around six hours to wait for my next flight, so I took my time. Dragging my bag on and off the connecting bus service was a real trial, but I refused to be hurried and moved as carefully as possible, resting as often as I could.

'If I can't manage my gear now, then how will I survive on this damn trek?' Once again, I was back to the relentless churning in my head, doubts to the fore. However, each hurdle climbed built my confidence as the day progressed.

I am a seasoned traveller, so some aspects of the journey were routine for me. Airports are familiar territory, and it was unusual for me to be confounded by such minor issues.

Mind you, hauling luggage around has been an ongoing problem for me in recent years since breaking tendons in both shoulders, necessitating extensive and prolonged treatment and operations.

It was just as well Sarah and I weren't going to be carrying our own supplies. That had been one of our main requirements when choosing our trip. Porters were essential.

Once on the first Air Maroc flight, my excitement began to build, and the two-and-a-half hours seemed to pass quickly.

The previous conversation with my fellow passenger had boosted my confidence. I felt secure in the knowledge that I was well informed about Factor V Leiden.

However, my back problem was constantly dragging me down, reminding me of the rigours to come, but I had made it this far on my own, so this was it.

'Grab this experience with both hands and enjoy it. You can do it!' My natural optimism was reviving even though my stomach was churning with anticipation. I was still nervous, but finally looking forward to the challenge to come.

I knew my friend would be anxious about many aspects of it, not to mention culture shock from her first experience of an Arabic country. It would seem so alien in many ways. I had to be strong and confident for her too.

I felt a real sense of responsibility for Sarah, in every way. From her enjoyment of the trek to her physical ability to complete it. I wanted to support her, and I sensed that her family had put me in the role of protector, a commitment I was ready and willing to accept.

As it turned out, Casablanca airport was a difficult place to keep your spirits up. It was about as far removed from my romantic notions as it could possibly be. There was no Humphrey Bogart waiting in the wings.

The international area looked clean, brightly lit and was bustling with rather exotically clothed men. I noticed very few women around, which makes most ladies feel, if not uncomfortable, then alert to our safety, and I was no exception. I was paying close attention to those around me.

Most Moroccan men wear the dress-like *djellaba* which, at that time of year, was made of rough cloth and was worn like a coat, over their usual clothes. Sometimes with pointed hoods hanging down the back, they were quite different from what I was used to seeing.

As a transfer passenger, I had no bag to retrieve, so, saying a prayer to the gods of luggage in the hope that mine would catch the onward flight, I followed the signs to the national part of the terminal.

Everything was written in French and Arabic, so I had to try and put Spanish out of my mind and concentrate on the long-forgotten French from my school days.

'*Muy bien*,' once again escaped my lips as I asked directions to my departure gate.

This ubiquitous Spanish expression drew some strange looks. Who was this blond woman, obviously

English (or German or Swedish; I have been mistaken for both) speaking Spanish in a French-speaking country? No wonder people seemed confused.

It took ages to wend my way down endless corridors, giving me time to feel excitement flooding my body. This was it, there could be no going back now.

Once I left the international section, I felt like I had gone down the rabbit hole in *Alice in Wonderland*. Suddenly everything seemed different.

Morocco wasn't a shock to me as I had been there before, but it was a big change to suddenly go from the cosmopolitan, antiseptic international atmosphere, into the very different local arena.

At least I hadn't had to brave the hordes of shouting taxi drivers that are usually found competing for business outside terminal buildings in the Arab world.

The decor became dark and dirty with grubby handprints around doorways and fixtures. Corridors were poorly lit and seemed to go on forever.

The departure area couldn't have been further away from a lounge if it tried. The seating was bare metal, uncomfortable and uninviting, set against dirty marble walls and floors with a dry fountain full of plastic bottles and bags in the centre.

There were lots of dispirited local people sitting about, surrounded by huge nylon bags overflowing with food and clothing. At least there were no live animals in evidence.

I tried hard to keep my spirits up for the next couple of hours as I waited for the rest of my trekking companions to arrive.

Knowing it was unlikely there would be power to recharge my Kindle, I had taken a light paperback with me and tried to read for a while.

99

Often, I got up and mooched about, keeping a sharp eye on my possessions, easing the stiffness in my back, gingerly feeling my left thigh in the hopes that the internal tingling was receding.

I didn't feel too bad at this point, bolstered by high doses of painkillers. However, I had decided to keep them for the daytime and give my body time to recover from them at night, so I was increasingly uncomfortable.

Mainly I watched with idle curiosity the comings and goings around me, all the while waiting to hear English voices echoing along the corridors, heralding the arrival of my fellow travellers.

Airlines don't often hand out meals these days, so I had taken my own supply of fruit, nuts and sandwiches to munch on, giving me something else to do to while away the time.

By eleven o'clock I was feeling very weary. Although we had only a brief half an hour flight over to Ouarzazate, it would be the early hours of the morning before we reached our hotel. I was sure it would be a dawn start the next day and reckoned that sleep would be rather a precious commodity for the next few days.

'Yeah, this is it. Just around this corner.' Voices echoed in the departure area as a group of excited, travel-weary Brits came bustling down the stairs. My heart was racing as I searched for my friend who, being short (not even quite 5ft tall), wasn't always easy to spot.

I was full of anticipation and relief that I was now going to be sharing this adventure with someone familiar to me.

'Trod, Trod, over here!' I called out her nickname, and several people looked round, seeming puzzled.

I spotted Sarah and enveloped her in a bear hug, feeling her relief that I was there as promised.

The reaction of her travelling companions, who looked curiously and then shrugged their shoulders with a slight knowing smile, made me realise she had been talking about me on the flight from London. No doubt our relationship, and how we met, had been put under the spotlight. My only hope was that I lived up to expectations.

Our group settled onto the deserted cafeteria chairs, twittering like a flock of birds. Alliances formed as Sarah sat down next to me, and we had a hurried update on all our news.

'Tell me the truth, how's your back? Have you been holding out on me?'

I hadn't wanted to transfer any of my angst to her, but, having kept her at arm's length, she was now determined to find out the strength of the problem while I was still trying to avoid the subject. The trek would expose my weaknesses and pain threshold soon enough without me having to spell it out.

'How do you feel? Are you excited, tired or what?' I asked, countering her question.

We were in a little bubble of our own, with a bond of friendship that excluded the others.

'I'm so relieved you're here. I was worried you might not make it,' Sarah declared, looking tired and a little dishevelled from her four-and-a-half-hour flight.

'It's been fun meeting everyone, and it all went smoothly at Heathrow, but I'm shattered now.'

Her bluster failed to cover her fears and doubts about the challenge ahead, or how we would cope with our respective physical limitations.

We were dragged out of our little world by a commanding Scottish voice.

'Gather round now, please. I need to give you all some information about the plans for our arrival in Ouarzazate and our departure tomorrow morning. Give us all a brief introduction to yourselves, starting with you, Dawne, as you haven't had the chance to meet everyone yet.'

Dropped in at the deep end by Angela, our trek leader, to whom I had only just managed a brief hello, I blurted out a couple of facts.

'Um, well, my name is Dawne, and I suppose you've already heard about me from my friend Sarah. Only the good bits are true.' There were a few chuckles. 'I've travelled from Mallorca and am supporting Thrombosis UK.' That was about all I could think of to say, but it seemed to be enough. Most people were similarly brief in their introductions, but it was hard to remember who was who.

We were all tired and apprehensive about what was to come, so we concentrated on listening to Angela giving us our instructions.

'I know it will be very late when we arrive, but we have an early start in the morning. Breakfast is at six o'clock with a seven o'clock pick up by the Moroccan team.'

Everyone groaned, but it was nothing more than I had expected. It wasn't supposed to be a holiday.

Turning to listen to a commotion nearby, I tuned into the French words.

'*Mais ou, si vous plait ?*' One of our guys was holding a rapid-fire conversation in French with the representative of Air Maroc, who was telling us our flight was undersubscribed. The airline intended to amalgamate it with the early one in the morning.

The discussion rapidly escalated into a full-blown argument with arms flailing and exclamations at top volume. As far as we were concerned, we needed to get our flight as scheduled.

The only concession we managed to gain was to join a flight to Marrakesh in an hour or so. It would divert first to our destination to drop us off. It was chaos. We didn't believe that this would happen or that our luggage would travel with us, and it seemed an unlikely solution to our dilemma.

It wasn't life-threatening, of course, but important for the smooth running of our plans to arrive in Ouarzazate that night. Our spokesman had done a sterling job of explaining that to the Air Maroc representative.

We were now trying to find the right gate for departure. Were we ever going to get there? There was a universal flagging of spirits and sighs of resignation from us all. A sense of "what will be, will be" prevailed. We were ready to bed down right there.

It was hard to concentrate on why we were there, in the midst of such an argument, but the one thing that kept me focused was thinking about the money mounting up in my Just Giving account.

Donations kept rolling in, along with sums raised in other ways, and the total on that first day of the trek stood at £3,500. I was ecstatic; it was far more than I could have hoped for.

This was the whole point; the funds I was raising would help Thrombosis UK to assist others. Having received so much support myself, I felt honour bound to complete the task I had chosen. Many people had been so generous that I felt a great weight of responsibility on my shoulders.

Head up, hat on. I was ready to conquer the desert. As I wrote in my diary the next day,

All I have to do now is get this trek trekked.

CHAPTER SEVEN
Day Two – First Steps

I was so tired, the trip from the airport to the hotel was a complete blur. My first impression was that we were in some sort of desert tourist resort. The one storey hotel looked quite modern, although the terracotta walls and arched windows and doorways hinted at another culture and style.

Reaching our room at three in the morning, we were exhausted. Despite being travel-weary, we were both over-excited to have finally arrived at the start of our adventure. We had been anticipating and fretting over it for months and were unable to resist chatting and catching up on all our news.

'What do you think of this place then?' I asked.

'I didn't know what to expect, but I love the traditional tiles in the bathroom. They are a gorgeous blue design. It's a shame I can't take any back with me. They'd look great at home.'

'A bit too heavy to cart around the desert for the next week,' I joked.

'It's more cosmopolitan than I thought it would be, but it doesn't quite live up to the hype, does it?'

'I didn't expect the hotel to be in the midst of renovations,' I agreed.

We arrived in the quiet hours of the night, and there were only a couple of the hotel staff around to greet us in the spacious, Berber tent-style lobby.

Carpeted with richly coloured rugs, with fabric draped from the ceiling, it was anything but European. It felt exotic and strange, yet behind that first facade, we found ourselves hurrying along echoing concrete corridors, past the hotel pool, which appeared to be in the

105

midst of a revamp with heaps of broken tiles all around its dusty perimeter.

I could smell the exotic night scents of oleander and jasmine, but we were hardly an appreciative audience, being more concerned with getting into our rooms for a few short hours of rest.

'Do you think we've remembered everything then?' I asked, speaking over Sarah. She was trying to remember which of us had agreed to bring what.

'I don't know, but I'm sure we'll find out soon enough.'

It had seemed daft for us both to bring all our trek requirements, so we had pooled our resources, although it seemed likely that we had doubled up on some things and, no doubt, missed out an essential item.

'How is your back now, Dawne? You went all quiet on me this week, and I've been really worried.' Sarah carefully approached the one subject I was keen to downplay.

'I didn't want to put you through the agonising I've been doing. I'm here and want to get on with it,' I replied, avoiding the question. 'How about you?'

'My stomach is churning already. I'm not sure we're up to this. I haven't done much training recently,' she wearily admitted.

'You were fit to go in September,' I enthused, attempting to bolster her flagging self-confidence.

'Don't you remember our sand walking attempts?' she giggled. 'What a load of rubbish.'

'Well, there are two of us to look out for, so I'm sure they will slow down for us,' I said, not necessarily believing it myself.

'Today is another day,' I joked, eyeing the clock, already perilously close to our scheduled six o'clock wake up call. 'Better try and get a bit of sleep. Nighty night. I'm so excited we're finally here together.' The sounds of light snoring confirmed that my companion was already in the land of Nod.

****

'Beep, beep, beep,' the alarm clock radio insistently chirruped through my sleep-deprived haze. It was a good job we'd noticed it sitting on the bedside table when we arrived.

'Wakey, wakey, Sarah,' I whispered, and it was no more than a minute or so before we both prised open our tired eyes. Looking over, I saw a grin steal across her face.

'Baggsy me first in the bathroom.'

'Oh, go on then,' I conceded, grateful for the few moments of privacy to roll myself carefully out of bed, checking my already pain ravaged body.

There was little time for introspection. I didn't want my friend to see the sorry state I was in as I swallowed the first of the day's regime of painkillers.

Strapping the brace around my stiff and aching back, it was hidden beneath my light cotton trousers and loose t-shirt; it wasn't obvious what I was wearing, and only my mate would know how I usually moved. No one else would realise my rigid gait and pained expression wasn't normal, or so I hoped. I was reluctant to share my situation with anyone if I could avoid it.

What would I do if I had managed to get all this way for nothing? I was worried about "Elf and Safety", knowing how ridiculous some of their rules can be, determined they were not going to get in my way.

Stubborn, maybe foolish? Yes, I lay claim to all of that, but the doctors had said 'go' so I was going, come hell or high water.

'Come on,' I said, chivvying Sarah along to the dining room to meet the other somewhat crumpled members of our group.

Having made some friends on the plane over to Casablanca before I joined the trip, she was ahead of me in the meeting and greeting department, taking great delight in introducing me properly to everyone.

'This is my mate, Dawne.'

'Oh yes, we've heard so much about you,' was the usual teasing reply.

'None of it is true,' I cried, nudging my pal sharply in the ribs.

'Oy!' she exclaimed, 'I only said good things you know.'

'I don't know about that; you sound like a right pair. I could hear you giggling from my room which, sadly, was next door to yours,' grumbled Angela, in her soft Scottish burr. She was representing Charity Challenge on our trek. We were in trouble already, both managing to look just a little sheepish. Talk about second childhood. A pair of fifty-something-year-olds getting a ticking off.

'OK!' shouted Angela over the excited chatter. Being short, she stood on a chair and waved her arms to capture our attention. 'We need luggage out in front of the hotel in ten minutes.' Brief and to the point, she came across as a lady used to be taken notice of. 'Our drivers will be there, ready to get your gear packed onto the jeeps for the trip to our start point. It's about five hours drive time into the desert.'

'What, no camels?' I whispered to Sarah.

108

'Thank goodness,' she replied, probably remembering our worried conversations about types of bags to take and whether or not wheelies could be carried on a camel.

I was greatly relieved that I wasn't going to look a complete prat for bringing wheeled luggage on a trek; essential for me as I wasn't able to carry a heavy pack on my back. Thank heavens for modern desert travel.

'Come on, Sarah, let's go choose a jeep, or a driver more like,' I quipped mischievously. 'Lawrence of Arabia might be out there waiting for us.'

'Picture time,' ordered Angela. 'I want you all in a group please, so we can get the "before" photos.'

That sounds bossy, but she had a way of phrasing things with a hint of humour that took the sting out of it. A small, compact woman, she was fit, experienced and comfortable in our current environment.

Ready to have some fun, but with no room for arguments, she was very much in charge, and I thought she would be a great trek leader.

'Before?' I whispered to Sarah, who was attempting to kneel at the front.

'Goodness knows what we'll look like afterwards, with no showers or clean clothes left after five whole days in the desert.'

It wasn't until we looked back at these photos and compared them with those we took on our return to Ouarzazate, that we realised Angela knew the toll the coming days would take on us all.

'Give your cameras to Ibrahim. I'm sure he will oblige us by taking photos for you.' He seemed a little overwhelmed as we all surged forward at once with a series of garbled instructions.

'Here, this is very simple.'

109

'Are we all in the picture?'

'Oops, can you take a pic with mine too?'

It was just as well they were digital and easy to use.

We laughed at Bibi's attempts to joke with us in his passable but somewhat fractured English, and he became our David Bailey for the duration. I overheard someone christen him Bibi, which seemed to suit him and distinguished him from other Ibrahims on the trip.

The "before" photo.

When I look back at that photo now, I can see that I looked pained, trying to stand up straight. I couldn't kneel in the front row and wasn't really tall enough to stand behind. Knowing Sarah as I do, I could see she was apprehensive, but I am sure to anyone else we looked like an excited bunch, eager to start our adventure.

Cliques were already forming while others remained aloof, but I had not yet had time to sort out names or personalities.

Perhaps I came across as a little standoffish, as I hadn't had the chance to form friendships on the journey over from England, while Sarah was already absorbed into the group, laughing and giving some backchat in response to banter about it.

We all appeared well prepared in sensible kit, with sun hats and lotions ready to go. The only jarring note was a couple of girls who wanted to stop and get some drinks to take with us, of the alcoholic variety. Alcohol is widely available in the tourist areas of Morocco, but spirits generally take second place to local beer. A bottle of vodka and mixers seemed a tall order.

'Who would need to drink vodka on a trek?' I whispered to my mate.

'I don't know,' she replied. 'I can't imagine that we'll have the energy for partying after walking all day.'

'We all need to be very focused. I'm concerned about dehydration,' added Angela, shaking her head and quite obviously wondering what they were thinking. 'I know it's meant to be fun, but bad heads are common after a day in the desert. It's hard to drink enough water, and alcohol only makes the matter worse.'

After a private chat, I'm happy to say that they took her advice in the way it was meant, and the girls turned out to be some of the most entertaining and committed members of our group.

For Sarah, the culture shock from her first experience of an Arab country must have been huge. We were winding through villages of mudbrick houses on dusty roads, being watched with great curiosity by the local children gathered outside their homes.

Even their outward appearance was unfamiliar as dusky brown faces peered out of doorways, dressed in what looked to us like the raggedy clothing of street urchins. Some ran alongside us, waving and holding hands outstretched as they called for gifts.

111

'Give, pens, money, please! Anything?' they shouted after us, some laughing, others sullen, as the trucks passed by.

Despite being jolted around, Sarah and the other two girls dozed off in the back seat. They had switched off from the onslaught of sights and sounds.

Tired and apprehensive, it had all become a bit much to take in. Although, goodness knows how they managed it because our driver was a good candidate for the Paris-Dakar rally. It was not supposed to be a race, and his overtaking manoeuvres on blind corners weren't much to anyone's liking. I spent most of the time hanging on tightly and muttering little prayers on the sharpest bends.

When the jeeps were loaded with our luggage, we had teamed up with two other trekkers who were looking a bit bewildered by the scramble for places.

Sarah, Polina and Jo were squashed together on the back seat, without much legroom, so I was relieved to have been unchallenged in my tentative request for the front seat. At least I could stretch my legs forwards, conscious as always of the need to keep them moving.

Knowing that we had a long journey in front of us, with this in mind, I was wearing Norahs (my nickname for compression socks. Norah Batty was an old Yorkshire woman from an English comedy programme who always wore such things). However, they were uncomfortable, and my feet kept slithering around in my sweaty hiking boots.

Until you have tried wearing pop socks in ninety-degree heat, you won't know what I mean. I pitied my tent mates when I peeled them off. Not even clothes pegs would keep the smell at bay.

Trying vainly to cushion the jolts from the bumps in the road, I was hanging onto the interior roof handle for all I was worth, wriggling about to ease the persistent pain in my back.

No doubt I had a somewhat strained expression on my face when we finally stopped for a comfort break.

'Are you coming to stretch your legs and have a look around?' asked Sarah.

Lagging behind, I was keen that no one should see me climbing stiffly down from the jeep.

'Are you OK?' I carefully stood and attempted to stretch. 'I know you're hurting, but you wouldn't tell me anyway, would you? I can see it in your face.' My grimace was answer enough.

We had pulled up outside a shop selling scarves and trinkets along with the delicious local sweet and syrupy mint tea; it was a good pick-me-up.

I was ready for another painkiller, swallowed down with a gulp of water and a handful of fruit and nuts to line my stomach. I didn't need to add digestive problems to my current list of woes.

'Come on,' said Sarah, taking my arm in an attempt to help me along. 'Let's go and sample the mint tea and try on a few scarves.'

We went to join the rest of the group, milling about inside the surprisingly cool mudbrick house.

'I fancy the red and white checked one myself, or maybe that long blue Berber one. What do you think?' she asked as we walked through several rooms with tables displaying local trinkets, into the main area, draped with multi-coloured lengths of material against the bare terracotta walls.

Several of our companions were standing patiently as local boys wound scarves around their heads in the traditional Berber style as protection from the burning sun.

It was rude to giggle as the "assistants" were taking it very seriously, but they soon realised they might make a sale if we all had a good laugh over how odd we looked, swathed in yards of fabric.

Before leaving, with colourful scarves stuffed into our daypacks, we had to face the inevitable queue for the hole in the ground toilet. What an experience and not in a good way.

Unaccustomed to the powerful stench that assaulted our noses, the smell that wafted out in the mid-day heat, across the courtyard, was unforgettable. However, the basic concrete rooms, with their open doorways and tap with a hose attached for washing away the offending waste, were to become a common sight.

We all came out scrabbling for the sanitary hand gel we carried in our packs, hoping to keep stomach bugs at bay for the coming trip.

Back on the road again, we whizzed along a flat plain with the majestic Atlas Mountains shimmering in the distance. A mirage caused by the searing heat made the road ahead appear to be covered in water. With the magnificent backdrop of jagged peaks silhouetted against the clear blue sky, the mist covering the foothills made them seem almost ethereal. It was a magical sight.

My appreciation was short-lived. I was in constant pain as my back had stiffened up from sitting in the same position for hours on end, punctuated only by frequent toilet stops, requiring me to climb awkwardly down from the truck. It was essential though, as we were drinking lots of water to keep hydrated, and it gave me the chance to stretch my legs properly.

With the hole in the ground toilet experience in mind, it was now time to try going bush.

For me, it was no joke. Squatting behind a patch of scrubby vegetation at the roadside meant I was immobilised as my back locked up. I had to resort to rolling forwards onto my knees to preserve my modesty before attempting to get up again. It was proving to be a long day.

The hotel had kindly given us each a packed lunch to take with us, and we were more than ready for it as we stopped, some five hours out of Ouarzazate. Sitting under the shade of an acacia thorn tree, we wrestled with the tin of tuna we had been given.

'What am I meant to do with that?' exclaimed Sarah, with a grimace. Showing her the ring pull top, it didn't seem such a bad idea after all, but you try using flatbread as a scoop to get the tuna out of the tin.

Hardboiled eggs and bologna sausage plus an orange completed lunch, by the end of which I had my first dirty t-shirt, covered in oily splashes and bits of eggshell, smelling of fish, eggs and oranges. The only alternative was to remain hungry.

'I didn't like those eggs much, did you?' asked Sarah.

'How do you mean?' I replied. 'Mine was OK. Good energy for this afternoon's exertions.'

'Mine tasted a bit weird, but then I've never tried a Moroccan hardboiled egg before,' she laughed. Those words would come back to haunt her.

Hoisting ourselves back into the jeep, we were on the road again, but I began to tire of the views in front of us and turned to observe my travelling companions.

The driver was Moroccan, dark and brooding, monosyllabic despite our best attempts to ask him questions in French. Perhaps he only spoke Arabic? He certainly preferred to keep himself to himself, and I was glad he could keep his full attention on the road ahead.

I couldn't see the girls sat in the back, but they had been a little chattier in the last hour or so as we exchanged information about where we were from and why we were trekking. Everyone agreed that this was going to be quite testing.

Polina had come all the way from Australia to join our group. I think she had tied it into a more extensive tour of Europe. I looked forward to learning more about her and her background. She was born in St Petersburg and lived there as a child. Though a little shy, I was sure she would have more to say as she got used to us.

Jo was determined to achieve this challenge before turning thirty in a few months. Was she proving a point to herself? I hoped to find that out over the coming days.

I later found out that Jo was suffering from tendonitis in her feet, and the only cure was complete rest. I admired her tenacity as she was in pain throughout our trip and probably munched as many painkillers as I did. She was one of the few people I confided in about my problems. I didn't admit how bad I felt, as I was rather overawed by her fortitude.

The last hour of our drive was exhilarating but very scary. The four of us were strap hanging, trying to hold on. We were off-road by now, and our driver raced over the sand and gravel tracks, bouncing and jolting between the ruts, competing against the other jeeps along the trails as we moved deeper into the increasingly barren desert landscape. Windows tightly closed against the dust clouds rising from our convoy, we left a plume in the air, marking our way onwards.

By the time we stopped, I was desperate to get out. The exhilaration of our race had worn off as the pain in my back intensified with the bouncing around. Groaning quietly to myself, I climbed stiffly down.

'This is it, Trod,' I whispered, hoping the use of her daft nickname would lift our spirits as we struggled into our daypacks. We were both somewhat overwhelmed with the harsh reality of our undertaking, and Sarah was looking uneasy and uncomfortable but blustered back.

'Come on, Bossy One. Let's get started,' and forged ahead along the dusty track towards our first dune.

We set off with Bibi and The Boss (another Ibrahim, our Moroccan trek leader) leading the way and Angela bringing up the rear beside us.

I experienced a rush of anticipation and excitement, tempered by the ever-present stiffness and pain from my back as underused muscles were forced into action.

As it was mid-afternoon, the temperature was still high and the sun intense, although we were to come to appreciate this time of day as better for walking once the extremes of midday had passed. However, I found the sun blindingly bright, and sunglasses were essential, along with hats and sunscreen for faces and any other exposed body parts.

I had chosen to stay in long cotton trousers and a t-shirt. Shorts were quickly pulled on by some, as we started to sweat our way up the first dunes. However, I found the thought of balancing precariously in the soft sand was too much to contemplate. Also, I had experienced Mallorcan summers, with temperatures sometimes over a hundred degrees. I knew that stripping off in the heat doesn't always make you feel cooler. Desert dwellers are usually completely covered up.

I felt full of trepidation about how I would cope, so I stayed back, along with Sarah who seemed overwhelmed by what we had started.

'How long are we walking for?' I asked Angela.

Her accent giving away her origins, she replied, 'Och, it's only about an hour and a half or so to get us into camp. Just a taste of the desert to get us away from the tracks and loosened up after that interminable drive,' she laughed.

Somehow, I couldn't get into a rhythm at all. I had only decided at the last minute to take two hiking poles and wasn't accustomed to using them in the soft and shifting sand. Deeply uncomfortable, unable to relax and fighting my body rather than working with it, I was on the verge of tears, trailing the poles behind me.

We had walked only a short way, but I wanted to feel at one with the landscape. All I could sense was the intense heat, rising from the ground through my sturdy boots, making my feet swell. Rivers of sweat ran into my eyes from underneath my sunhat, which was essential wear, despite finding it made my head swelter, along with the thick hanks of hair I had shoved up under it in a vain attempt to keep it from the back of my neck.

However, I was exactly where I wanted to be. On the ridge of a tall dune, climbing in a line of trekkers towards the summit. That is an image I have always had in my mind, and there I was, achieving one of my ambitions.

I was very emotional when we finally reached the top, and I stopped to rest on my poles, feeling a lot of angst and fears about coping.

Taking time to soak up the vista of dunes fading into the distance in front of us, I could see occasional scrubby thorn bushes struggling up through the sand. I was awestruck, wondering at the landscape in the harsh desert sunlight. It was such a contrast to anything I had seen before. Despite feeling intense pain, I began to see the effort was going to be worth it.

Of course, that brief respite put me even further behind everyone else, but neither Nia (our young Welsh medic) nor Angela seemed unduly perturbed at this point.

I discovered the poles helped me get some purchase by digging them deep into the grainy sand, just ahead of my feet, then leaning on them to haul myself further up the steep slope. I was in a rhythm of sorts.

Sarah and I were immediately spotted as stragglers, and we soon had help and encouragement from both Angela and Nia.

My mate is less than five feet tall, and her short legs and small feet kept sinking, so she needed some assistance to get the hang of it. I was stiff and awkward, constantly favouring my back while attempting to push on the poles to give me leverage. All I needed was time.

'So, you are one of the people I have to keep a special eye on,' continued Nia, following our introduction to one another over the strain of getting me over those first few ridges. I laughed at that, wondering if she had been talking to Angela about our antics last night.

'You mentioned on your medical form that you have Factor Five Leiden. Tell me about that and how it affects you. I need to know what I should look out for if you are having a problem.'

I was more worried about my back at this point but decided not to mention it for fear of being excluded from the rest of the trek at this late stage. I was determined to handle the pain and suffer in silence.

'Oh, I don't anticipate any issues,' I blithely replied, going on to explain about the two blood clots I had, and how I prepare before travelling. As I had accomplished the flights without any hiccups, I reckoned the daily exercise would keep me from having any difficulties.

119

'You seem to be well informed. You certainly know more than I do about Factor Five Leiden, and how to cut down the risk of clotting again.'

'I feel knowledge is power,' I explained, and we made an agreement that I was to talk to her should I have any worries.

Nia was a fun, lively woman in her twenties, spectacularly well-travelled with lots of tales to tell, and we were to spend many hours slogging along at the back of the pack, chatting and joking about our experiences.

'It must be lovely to travel with such a good mate. You know each other so well and maybe spot things I might miss. At least I get a warning of anything untoward.' she said.

'I know what you mean,' I replied. 'Sarah sometimes faints in difficult situations, and she's not so good in the heat, so we'll have to watch out for that.'

'Blimey, maybe a desert trek wasn't such a good choice.' I spluttered with laughter at that.

We were walking on the flat at this point. Descending the dune had turned out to be as much a trial for me as going up. Whilst everyone else, Sarah included, picked up speed and surfed through the soft sand as it propelled them downwards, I was left behind, trying not to jar my back, and carefully placing my feet to keep control.

We weren't far from our camp, but as I looked at my friend, who was some metres ahead, I turned to Nia in a panic.

'I think she's got a problem. Sarah's going to faint. Quick!' which sent her running to her side, at which point my intrepid pal threw up all over Nia's boots. By the time I got to them, poor Sarah was in the throes of a violent vomiting attack.

Our medic was calm and matter of fact as we sat together for some time while my friend lost the contents of her stomach.

I was horrified. My poor mate looked bewildered, heaving and retching, sweating from the heat and the effort. What a start to our adventure.

Despite her protestations, she was taken the few hundred yards into camp in the back of the jeep which had come out to us. She looked very green and sick.

'What's happened? Is Sarah OK?' everyone asked as they crowded around us.

'We've put your gear into our tent, so you're with us,' Jo said, which was very reassuring.

Sarah was in no mood to care. Around the back of the medical tent, she continued to vomit every few minutes, despite being given anti-nausea medication, which she brought right back up again, along with the recently eaten lunch, including the dodgy egg.

'Please go, Dawne. I want to be on my own,' she muttered, obviously not needing an audience.

'Don't worry, I'll stay with her,' Nia offered, so I took myself off to organise our sleeping bags, hoping fervently that she would start feeling better soon.

Afterwards Sarah told me that she kept on thinking 'Oh no. Day One, and I'm sick to my stomach. What have I done? What am I doing here?'

It was hard to join in with things that evening, and everyone was subdued, worried about our companion and somewhat daunted by the task we were undertaking. At least it stopped me from feeling sorry for myself.

I found it difficult to move around, ducking through openings and lowering myself onto the ground by our bags. Fortunately, everything was already set up by the

Moroccan team. We came into a readymade camp, for which I was incredibly grateful.

We had a square of tents, two each for men and women, plus a separate one for Nia and Angela. The cooks, porters and guides were a little apart, some choosing to sleep outside or even in the trucks.

A short distance away, lurking like silent sentinels standing guard, were the toilet and shower tents.

As for peeing over the hole in the ground, you do not want to go there. Suffice to say that I almost brought the canvas down once or twice, having to hang onto one of the poles to haul myself back upright from a squatting position. I was in so much pain that I felt unable to support my weight with my back in such a state. It sounds like proper slapstick comedy, but it's not funny when it's happening to you.

Sarah didn't manage to join us that first evening, as we crowded around the tables and chairs set up in the centre of our encampment, queuing up for our food and taking the opportunity to get to know one another better.

There isn't much meat available out in the wilds, but our food was hearty and filling, if mainly vegetarian. Soup starters were delicious and satisfying, including lentils and other pulses to bulk them up.

Often the main course was a kind of stew called tagine, with or without some stringy and tough chicken, accompanied by pasta, potatoes or couscous. At least we had plenty of carbohydrates to give us energy. I found it hot, tasty and filling, but it wasn't to everyone's liking.

The cooks and porters were all friendly and prone to having a good laugh at our expense. The language was a barrier. However, French was spoken by the majority of the ground crew, so we usually managed to communicate fairly well. I used my schoolgirl French with more and more confidence as the week progressed, but Arabic was beyond all of us.

We didn't feel much like partying that first night. Darkness came early, and the temperature dropped quickly, so we were all ready to rest and regroup for the coming challenge. The majesty of the desert night was lost on us.

Once Sarah stopped being sick, she crawled into her sleeping bag and slept like a log. It seemed like the best medicine, although I worried long into the night about whether or not she would be able to continue in the morning. I have never seen someone be so violently ill for so long and be fully functional the next day.

I was unable to get comfortable on the bedrolls provided. Although more cushioned than I had expected, my back pain intensified as the night progressed, as I had decided to give my body a rest from the painkillers for a few hours.

It was important to me that no one else realised how concerned I was about my situation. So, I lay on my back, listening to the whispered conversations and the curious sounds of barking and strange grunting from the nocturnal animals busy in the night.

I found it hard to ignore the movements of the creaky canvas of our old-fashioned tents and eventually resorted to listening to music on my iPod to try and relax and forget my constant fretting.

'Stop it, Dawne,' I cautioned myself. 'You have made it this far the rest will be a piece of cake. You go, girl!'

With my cheerleader voice firmly ringing in my ears, I drifted off for a few hours of restless sleep before waking early to face our first full day of trekking.

123

CHAPTER EIGHT
Day Three – Carols and Crisps

To avoid the worst heat of the day, we needed to start walking early, and it was about half past five when the sun rose, and people began to move around. Their murmured conversations gradually overcame the clanging of pans coming from the kitchen tent.

The female cook was constantly in fits of giggles, so goodness only knows what was going on in there. She turned out to be our morning pick-me-up, laughing and joking with her workmates. Considering it was all coming out of little more than a canvas shelter, she provided us with amazing food. I never could pronounce her name though. To me, she became Chuckles.

Quietly, so as not to wake Sarah, I turned to Jo who was lying on one of the other sleeping mats.

'Was I dreaming last night, or did some carol singers stop by?'

'Yes,' she giggled. 'I seem to remember a zebra singing "Good King Wenceslas",' she added.

Yes, really. Just as we were settling down for the night, there was a flurry of activity outside. A couple of verses of a carol were followed by the appearance of a zebra and a Hello Kitty character. These turned out to be two fellow trekkers (I never did find out who) dressed in onesies. Goodness knows how they got such bulky gear into their limited weight allowance, but they were very funny.

Whispering so as not to wake Sarah, they performed a little jig and then buzzed off next door. We could hear the giggles from there too. It was a light-hearted end to a stressful day, and it was a shame my poorly friend missed it.

Another of our tent mates, Lou, could be quite comical, and that morning was a case in point, without her saying a single word.

She had a sleeping bag that produced my first proper belly laugh of the trip, as it was in the shape of a person with separate arms and legs; it looked hilarious. Lou was stretched out on her back, like a starfish, arms and legs akimbo. I only had to think of that to feel a smile creeping across my lips, even on the toughest of days.

That person-shaped sleeping bag.

'It's a good job it has zippers everywhere,' she whispered to us. 'It was warmer than I expected last night, and I had to let some air in.'

'Oh, me too. I came prepared, and it's not very cold at all.'

Three-season sleeping bags are designed to keep you warm at temperatures as low as zero, and it was nowhere near that, but it was a very chilly run to the toilet at that time of day.

Having showered before we left the hotel (was it only twenty-four hours ago? It already felt like an eternity), wet wipes came into their own that morning. I had yet to brave the shower.

It was another small, square tent, open to the skies as you stood over a pit and used a cup filled with a little water from a jerry can to sluice down. It was more than I had expected but only bearable in the evenings after it had warmed in the heat of the day.

Worming my way out of my bedding was a slow and painful business, so I kept very much to myself, waiting for a bit of privacy, and not joining in with the general banter.

I did overhear the boys complaining about Des, who was a dreadfully loud snorer. Well into his sixties, he was the elder statesman of the group, and it remained to be seen how much teasing he could stand.

Up to now, he had seemed rather serious and keen to tell us all how to do everything. As it turned out, he had a well-developed sense of humour, even when the fun was at his own expense. The Moroccans nicknamed him Moustache for obvious reasons.

The twins (our intrepid French speakers who sorted out our airport dilemma) ended up sleeping on mats outdoors, snuggled into their sleeping bags, each one looking like a chrysalis.

They had been an enigma to me so far, and I made a mental note to corner each of them later and try to get to know them a little better.

Moving like a geriatric snail, I emerged with my back brace snugly fitted beneath a clean, if crumpled shirt, bags repacked and ready for action just as Sarah woke up from a deep but healing sleep, so I left her to get organised.

Gathering my already rapidly depleting reserves of energy and plastering a smile on my face, I pushed aside the tent flaps and stepped outside to join everyone at breakfast.

Reluctant to come outside and join us yet, my mate poked her head out of the canvas doorway, reminding me of the Leaning Tower of Pisa, as she stretched forward to whisper in my ear.

'Can I borrow you for a few minutes, please? I know it's cold, but I feel so vile and smelly from yesterday. I want to have a bit of a wash. Will you come and hold my clothes and soap and stuff?'

'OK,' I replied, knowing how difficult it was to keep things clean and organised. 'I'll stand guard while you're in the shower.'

Sand gets into all those important little places, so it's best to keep your clothes off the ground. We had also been told to watch for bugs that may have crawled into bags, boots and anything else left lying around. We had all been careful to close everything the night before and to shake our boots before putting them on again.

Scorpions abound in the desert, and they are nasty creatures that can give a very painful, or even deadly, sting. You don't want to stand on one of those first thing in the morning.

I have to say that I'm a bit of a wimp about insects and was just praying I didn't have a close encounter with any of the desert varieties of spiders either, as they can be large, hairy and poisonous.

'Oh, my God!' Sarah gasped, as the frigid water hit her skin which was still warm from her night in a cosy sleeping bag.

I shivered in the chilly morning air, in sympathy with my brave friend, as I handed her clothes back, piece by piece. Once dressed, I gave her a quick hug and rubbed her arms briskly to try and bring a little warmth into her limbs. Frankly, I was amazed she was even up and about.

'How are you feeling?' was the question on all our lips as she finally came to join us, blinking in the bright sunlight.

'Not too bad,' she said, trying to make light of it.

'What do you reckon made you so sick?' I asked.

'Do you remember the boiled eggs from yesterday's packed lunch? I only ate one, and it tasted weird to me. I think that was it.'

Of course, various theories were bandied about all day as everyone offered their own opinion. The unaccustomed heat can make you feel bad, as can drinking insufficient water, the new surroundings, lots of things can have a dire effect. But *that* sick? I have never seen anyone become so ill and manage to get out of bed the next day. Perhaps her almost immediate reaction meant little of the bad egg stayed in her system. I have mentioned that Sarah is an incredibly determined lady, and she truly was that particular morning.

Concerned for her wellbeing, Nia asked if she wanted to ride in the jeep for a few hours.

'No!' was her spirited reply. 'I know it's going to be hot, but I won't feel right if I don't try and walk as far as possible.'

My gutsy friend was foregoing all special treatment, determined to join the rest of us on that day's trek.

'People haven't sponsored me to sit on my bum. I just need some energy bars and rehydration salts to get me going.'

As a safety precaution, they had a jeep shadowing us all day from a distance as there were no roads or tracks on our route. It was to meet us at our noon lunch stop, allowing anyone who felt unable to continue to hitch a lift for a few hours.

Breakfast was scrumptious. Heartfelt murmurs of appreciation rolled around our motley crew, as we queued up for freshly cooked, delicious Moroccan pancakes, which we smothered in jam, washed down with warming mugs of English style tea.

I was so relieved that we had proper tables and chairs as it was almost impossible for me to sit on the ground, restrained by my back brace, still trying hard not to let anyone other than Sarah know that it was part of my kit. She always knew when I was in pain, just by looking at me. A kind glance from her was worth more than a thousand words.

We were sharing everything, from blister plasters to energy bars and trail mix, our favourite blend of fruit, nuts and the occasional chocolate button.

'Can I take your gear outside for you?' Sarah asked. 'It's nearly eight o'clock, and the crew are waiting to pack up the tents and load the jeeps.'

She sounded upbeat but already looked a little worn around the edges. It was typical of her to think of me first, something I hope I do in return. We were so close. Deep down, I felt sorry for her but knew I would embarrass her by showing my emotions.

By the time we straggled out of camp, our crew had tidied the area, sorted everything and left us to it. They were very efficient.

Setting off that morning, we waved a cheery 'goodbye' to the small bunch of children who had been watching us from a distance. Their dirty faces and scruffy appearance were at odds with their ready smiles and intense curiosity at our antics. Chattering amongst themselves like a flock of starlings behind our backs, we only caught their silent, shy grins, which remain imprinted on my memory. These "watchers" often appeared out of nowhere and hung around in the background, surveying the scene. You're never alone in Africa.

'It's such a shame you didn't see the sunrise this morning. It was so beautiful, full of colour.'

'I wasn't noticing anything, to be honest. Breakfast was enough of a challenge,' my friend replied wearily.

'Oh, you should have seen it. I went to the toilet early and, on the way back, ended up standing for ages.'

I had been spellbound by the orange hues of the sky, as the sun came up like a ball of flame. It was a view only possible in the desert or at sea, where the horizon is uncluttered by buildings or anything else for that matter. It had made me feel calm and insignificant, knowing that this was one sure immutable fact in an otherwise topsy turvy world.

Mentally gathering our resources, we knew it was going to be a long, tough day. By half past eight the sun was rising quickly, above a mist that drifted in a narrow band, close to the ground.

Dawn had been much earlier, but now, as the cold, damp night air met with the heat of the sand warmed by the sun, it caused this almost ethereal effect, like clouds of smoke.

'You know you won't be giving up if you hitch a lift in the truck for an hour or two when it gets really hot,' I mentioned, cautious of Sarah's feelings.

'Yeah, I know, but I'm OK. I want to walk all of this if I possibly can,' she replied, as defiant as ever. 'More to the point, how are you feeling?'

'Oh, I'm alright,' I said, aware that my mate would just ignore me, realising I couldn't bring myself to admit to any weakness.

'You know I'm here,' she said kindly. 'It's just as well we watch out for each other.'

I promised myself to keep an eagle eye on her, all the same. Knowing each other so well, you sometimes need someone close to confide in. We were both aware of such mundane things as each other's toilet needs, a thing of great importance, having to use bushes throughout our trek.

Sarah's system was messed up from her bout of sickness, and we both always needed to pee because of the amount of water we were drinking.

They say that women go to the bathroom in pairs, and it was certainly true in our case. A well-timed offer of a roll of loo paper is greatly appreciated when you're balancing precariously, trying not to wee on your boots. And there is nothing worse than sand in your toilet roll.

Water was just about the only thing I was carrying as I had realised my full-size daypack was too much for my back. Luckily, I had a smaller backpack that I had been using as a handbag when travelling.

We needed four litres of water a day whilst walking, plus drinks at lunchtime, tea and in the evening, so I had pared things down to the barest minimum, only carrying two litres of water to get me through to the next break.

I had decided to do without almost everything else. Glucose tablets for energy and toilet roll were my only concessions, being small and light.

Sarah kindly offered to take care of our precious trail mix. We were like Jack Spratt and his wife, picking over this particular bag of treats, one of us liking raisins, the other preferring peanuts – between us we would forage our way through a bagful every day. When we came across the occasional chocolate button, it was a no-holds-barred fight for that delicious, melted morsel to roll around our parched mouths.

'Yeah, dunes!' The gleeful cry came drifting back from the front of our group to my spot at the rear, where I was still struggling to get into my stride.

I felt a real sense of excitement, and my heart beat faster in anticipation. We quickened our pace, sending trickles of sticky sweat down my sides.

Dune walking to start our day. It would be tough. Most people visualise sand dunes when they think of the desert, and we were no exception. In reality, there are many types of terrain, but those slowly shifting crescents are the archetypal image we have in our heads when the Sahara gets mentioned. Along with visions of turbaned Berbers charging towards us on snorting, sweating horses, the exotic and dark-eyed men flourishing ceremonial swords and whisking us off to who knows where. In my imagination, anyway.

It was brilliant. Sarah got to grips with things and was forging ahead, tackling them with gusto. Of necessity, I took a more measured approach. The soft sand constantly dragged me downwards. I kept slipping and sliding and needed momentum to get up and along the ridges.

Thank goodness for the little gadgets on the bottom of my poles. I had put ski umbrellas on as they are much larger than those used by walkers and, once the poles were planted firmly into the sand, they supported my weight, and I used my shoulders to push upwards instead of my poor, aching back.

With my heart pumping from the effort, sweat dribbling from underneath my precious sun hat, I frequently stopped, ostensibly to admire the view but in reality, to rest and reorganise.

Learning to cope with dune walking.

The view of dunes in an endless vista, rolling towards the distant horizon, certainly made the stops worthwhile, but they were also a necessity as I gathered up strength, often readjusting my pack to ease aches and pains. I was using muscles I didn't know I had. It wasn't just my back causing problems. I suspected everyone was in some discomfort. None of us was accustomed to this sort of exertion on a daily basis.

At this point, I had no worries about whether I was up to the task; I was filled with a stubborn determination to see it through. There was no going back now.

Nia and Angela were rapidly becoming my constant companions, and I was starting to get to know a bit about them.

Nia, our medic, was light-hearted and constantly encouraging. She was full of stories about her travels and kept me thoroughly entertained.

Angela likewise. An enthusiastic ski guide in winter and trek leader in summer, we had lots of common ground and experiences to draw on. My background in hospitality and catering meant I had a similar stock of outrageous tales to tell.

Once we had slogged through the dunes, the landscape began to change, and we dropped to a lower level into a dried-up watercourse.

The Boss had called a rest stop to give us some information about the area we were passing through.

'This riverbed, he will be flashed full when the rain comes.' His English was great, if inventive.

Wrapped in his traditional blue Berber headgear and fully covered from the sun, he looked quite dashing, using his walking staff to direct our attention to points of interest. Omar Sharif sprang to mind, or maybe Laurence of Arabia.

The surrounding area looked as if it had not seen water for years, but when the rains come, they are harsh and fast. It was hard to imagine the desert would be green even for a short while. Our dusty crew sat around The Boss, trying to envisage great muddy torrents gushing over our feet.

Already hungry and thirsty, snacks and water came out as we compared aches and pains, caught between the pictures conjured from our imaginations and the reality of our demanding trek.

'It's like walking on giant crisps,' exclaimed Sarah as we continued on. 'Weird.' Many of us stopped to prod at the big flakes of mud, dried in the intense heat.

'It's an odd sensation. They're dry and crispy, but at least they're a rest from the soft sand,' I remarked, grateful for the change in terrain. I was trudging on with my head down to avoid any slips or trips which would jolt my back.

The Boss.

'Is my neck covered?' asked Sarah, taking care to keep her English rose complexion protected from the intense sun. The temperature was climbing into the nineties, even though it was not yet ten o'clock in the morning. We had only been going for a couple of hours before this short stop.

We started to join up with other people, comparing stories of the exploits which had led to our group being on this particular trek. I was glad to see everyone was keeping a close eye on my mate, applauding her tenacity. The heat, walking conditions and the unaccustomed environment were tough on all of us, but she was starting out in the worst way, still dehydrated from her intense bout of sickness the night before.

I am just an ordinary person, unaccustomed to feats of daring or bravery. I had expected to have to dig deep for reserves of energy to carry on with this challenge, but the emotional toll came at me out of left field as I tripped and almost fell.

'Are you OK?' my ever-observant friend called, suddenly dropping back beside me. 'You stumbled, how is your back?'

I looked at her, gulping back the tears which were never far from the surface, nerves screaming from the sudden, sharp jolt. Doubts rushed in at every available opportunity. Was I a hero or fool? I didn't know any more, and I could see that Trod was also full of apprehension about our undertaking.

What were we doing out in the desert? Both of us under the weather, and lacking in confidence about our abilities? Would anyone see us for what we were? I certainly felt like a fraud for rashly declaring I was up to this. Perhaps it was time for another painkiller?

'OK, yes, OK,' I lied to Sarah, knowing full well she could see right through me. 'Could you just sort out my water tube, please?'

Hoping to catch a quick break without attracting attention, we untangled it from the bladder in my daypack. It often came loose or got caught up in the straps. The stop, however brief, gave me a chance to regroup, rest a little and get myself back under control.

'More to the point, how are you doing?' I asked, deflecting the question. Feeling sorry for myself wasn't going to get this trek trekked.

Pulling myself up by the proverbial bootstraps, introspection over, on we went, crunching along.

Finding some small patches of shade beside the dry riverbed, we all took brief stops to take a long drink of water, re-apply sunscreen or readjust clothing.

I know it's essential to cover up in the sun so full-length cotton trousers and long sleeves were the order of the day even though my shirt was stuck to me. However, there were already lots of sunburned arms and legs amongst us.

Sweaty and sticky, we trudged on, back into an area of low dunes, until an apparition floated into view in the distance. Was it a tent, a truck, or a mirage before us? Speculation was rife, and the mystery gradually unfolded until we arrived at a jeep with a food table already laid out for lunch, plus an open-sided canvas shelter for us to rest in for a couple of hours in the shade.

Whilst the temperatures were high, it was a dry heat and not too uncomfortable. Mind you, my time in southern Spain has adjusted my body to summer temperatures above one hundred degrees, so I was in a better position than some in our group. Sarah looked worn out, which was hardly surprising.

We crashed out onto the carpets laid out in the shadow of the tent; stretched out together like a litter of tired puppies only smellier and not so cute.

We managed some fun and frivolities though. As I've mentioned before, wherever you go in Morocco there will be "watchers", even in the most remote places. An impromptu market stall appeared, as if from nowhere, with young girls selling a few homemade trinkets and jewellery.

Shyly peeking up at us and whispering amongst themselves, the ensuing laughter put us in our place. Thinking we were properly attired for desert trekking, our outfits were the source of much hilarity for them, swaddled as they were in layers of colourful cotton.

Angela, modelling one of her purchases.

The men remained in the background, looking mistrustful of us and carefully guarding the women.

Lunch was a kind of vegetable tagine with scrambled eggs cooked through it to give us energy. Most of the meals included some variation of this dish, the name of which refers to the traditional cooking pot, which is made of terracotta with a deep base covered by a funnel-shaped top and often highly decorated.

Of course, needs must out in the desert, so the fancy utensils were not in use, but the delicious stew was frequently served up, full of vegetables in a tasty sauce and sometimes meat if available. Poor cuts respond well to slow cooking. Served with potatoes, rice or pasta, it was good, filling sustenance.

'Yuk!' was Sarah's verdict, feeling more than usually wary of any egg-based foods. Understandable. However, it was hot and tasty and would keep us going until dinner.

My pal was in fairly good shape, and most of us were in high spirits, although I wasn't moving easily, finding that even the shortest stop allowed my back to stiffen up. It was difficult to get comfortable on the ground, so I took to walking slowly in the small patches of shade around our temporary camp.

Realising that, once again, there was sand in my boots, I stepped onto the heels to pull them off.

'Oh no!' I gasped, looking down in horror. 'It's come apart,' I added, wondering whether to giggle or cry, watching the back of my boot flapping in the wind. Carefully bending down to lift it to eye level, I realised everyone was watching me, stood on one leg, some yards in front of the tent. The leather upper had parted from the sole. I was mortified. What a thing to happen.

Many ink miles are used to encourage trekkers to buy good footwear and wear it in properly. Mine were certainly that. Ten years old and veterans of many a Sunday hike, they were leather which I prefer in the heat to modern synthetic materials. Some of my companions were regarding the offending boot with amusement and others with exasperation.

'Are they even proper walking gear?' asked one of the twins in his cut-glass accent. Up went the hackles on the back of my neck.

'Of course. I've done many a long mile in these. They only need a bit of glue,' I reasoned.

'How about gaffer tape?' suggested Angela

Gaffer tape saves the day.

The perfect answer. Something every well-prepared woman carries in her handbag or backpack. I'm not joking. A small torch, penknife, length of string and a roll of gaffer tape will rescue a well-organised female in most situations. Help was at hand.

So, my boot was duly strapped up, with my foot inside. It didn't move, and I was sure it would be OK until we got to camp, convinced that one of the older trucks would have a pot of glue stashed somewhere around, amongst other essential tools.

Feeling a tad foolish, I took up my customary spot at the rear of our party and got moving again for what turned out to be a three-hour slog across a huge plain of dark, hard-packed sand towards distant hills and dunes. There wasn't even a tree to break the monotony.

Funnily enough, I found it exhilarating. There were wide vistas in front of us and vast expanses of blue sky above, the desert floor shimmering like a lake in the distance. Sadly, there wasn't any water to be seen when we got there; it was a mirage.

The necessary toilet stops now had to be accomplished with the forbearance of us all. Someone would drop back, squat and hope no one looked back. You could hardly call them comfort stops, but that was how we began to refer to the whole process. It was a matter of trust. The whole group looked out for each of its members, slowing up as one lagged behind, ensuring they re-joined us.

In her preparatory talk, Angela had suggested that we needed to work together. Some walk slowly, some faster. There needed to be a mid-ground we could all accept. The aim was for us all to complete this, and it would mean taking care of one another, not competing or moaning about lack of pace.

It had begun to happen already. Everyone was watching out for Sarah, especially Bibi (the keeper of our cameras at any photo opportunity), who would quietly shoulder her daypack towards the end of each section of walking. Accustomed to these treks, he knew that tiredness creeps up and robs you of any reserves of energy, and he could see that she didn't have any, having been so sick. We all pulled together. It was a good feeling.

The hard-packed sand eventually gave out to an area that reminded me of salt pans. It was very flat and dazzling white in the sun, punishing for tired eyes.

We had a long, long slog to our campsite, set on a low plateau with the vastness of this desert all around us. It was a featureless vista and so awesome I felt almost insignificant.

It was a relief to trudge into our camping ground and see it was all prepared for us. Sarah was alongside me as we finally arrived, way behind the bulk of the party who were already busy showering and getting organised.

'Come on, Trod, it'll be dark soon. Let's go straight for a shower.'

'OK,' came the tired reply. 'I don't fancy it much, but it will be nice to get clean.' Rummaging in our packs to find soap and towels, we were desperate to remove some of the desert dust with a cupful of very welcome lukewarm water.

By the time we were sorted out, it was already dark. The sky had changed through every shade of orange as night fell.

While waiting outside the shower tent, I couldn't help but marvel at the extravagance of the colours, stretching out into the distance, fading into a deep, velvety blackness, reinforcing my feeling that I was just a speck in the universe. What a sight for our sore eyes.

Majestic desert sunset.

I need to wash out some clothes,' Sarah said sheepishly. The sickness had played havoc with her digestion, so we used our biodegradable soap liquid to rinse some things through by torchlight. Believe me, it was no easy task, but friends stick together through thick and thin.

My mate looked worn out and overcome by the minutia of camping. Every little job is so much harder to accomplish with only basic gear at hand, and we were a weary and somewhat careworn pair who eventually joined the others for dinner.

I had removed my back brace, which now hung in our tent, literally dripping with sweat from the heat and exertions of the day. Swallowing a couple more painkillers, I began to wonder if I would soon start to rattle.

We compared tales of woe. Jo had tendonitis in her feet. I felt humbled by her stoicism; I couldn't imagine how much pain she was in as she swallowed as many tablets as she could safely stomach.

'Beep, beep, beep,' a computerised chirrup, alien in the desert environment. Yes, really. In this day and age, we seem to feel the need to be attached to a phone at all times. We had been warned that communications would become difficult as we trekked further out, but, at this point, I could still receive and send a text. It felt good to be able to reassure Bernie I was holding up OK.

'Give me your boot,' ordered Bibi, disappearing off into the depths of a truck, the toolbox overflowing with useful bits and pieces and, presumably, some glue. Some minutes later, he reappeared with it held triumphantly over his head. The Boss immediately grabbed hold of it and jammed it underneath the leg of the dinner table to serve as a weight overnight for the glue to do its job. I knew they would have the technology to rebuild my precious hiking boot.

'We will be walking up and over a rocky plateau tomorrow,' The Boss said, giving us information about the next day. We were due to trek even further, so it promised to be a long and testing trial of our strength. The extra exertion needed for that kind of terrain was going to push us all to our limits, especially me with my dodgy back.

With half an ear on his instructions, I realised that Sarah was coming in for some light-hearted teasing about the events of yesterday, borne out of relief that she was still with us.

'I wondered what the heck I had got myself into,' she confessed as we got ready for bed.

My concerns about being at the rear of the party had proved unfounded. No one seemed unduly concerned, being more encouraging than critical. Most people had, at some time or another, dropped back to have a chat. We swapped stories of fundraising and why we were out there, facing the elements. I was starting to feel more a part of the group and beginning to sort out individual personalities.

The twins were brothers in their early thirties who seemed intent on complaining about most things and keeping themselves apart, walking with their iPod earbuds firmly in place. That was no way to get to know the rest of the party, but they seemed to have little interest in us.

Lou, Toni, Debs and Becky seemed to be our jokers, often accompanied by Nick the Giggler (aka Nicnoc). Their humour spilt over to entertain us all during the week.

Many of us had some kind of mascot with us. It may only have been a scruffy stuffed animal, but they all meant something.

Becky carried a small doll of the character Woody from the *Toy Story* film. He was a long-legged cowboy, and he was photographed wherever she travelled. Spotting Woody in amongst tree branches or halfway up a sand dune often made us laugh at the odd expression on his face.

Des was our elder statesman, used to doing these kinds of challenges, having raised thousands of pounds for the British Heart Foundation.

He was the other member carefully watched over, having had a varied history of heart problems and operations. He was an amazing guy and, despite his seriousness, was not averse to sending himself up so that he won the affection of us all, and we adopted him as another mascot.

Everyone had something to offer the party, although some came out of their shells more than others. There was almost universal interest in the tale of how Sarah and I first met and our meeting again over twenty-five years later. It makes me appreciate how special our friendship is and how lucky we are to have found one another again.

I'm not sure if my friend felt the same way at this point as I was somewhat taciturn, directing most of my energy towards completing the trek and controlling the pain in my back without letting anyone else know about it. She bore the brunt of my concerns, but, equally, I hoped I was supporting her in other ways.

'What time is it?' she whispered, over post-dinner mint tea. 'Can I go to bed yet?

'It's half past eight, and we were already in bed at that time last night,' I whispered back.

145

'I'm exhausted.'

'Oh, me too,' I readily agreed.

Our bodies were worn out. It's all very well pushing yourself for a strenuous hike on a Sunday and having the week to recover. It is quite another thing to get up and do the same the next day and the next. We were all beginning to feel exhausted. Everyone felt the same, and sleeping bags were waiting for us to snuggle into.

In the meantime, Nia was keeping a sharp eye on her flock, patiently dealing with a line of people forlornly waiting outside her tent, hoping she could tend to some nasty blisters, along with other relatively minor issues.

I had to laugh at myself as I carefully tried to wriggle into my sleeping bag and find a comfortable position. Houdini might have made a better job of it. I was so fearful of wrenching my back that I must have made quite a sight as I gingerly gathered all the things I might need but, once settled in, I could tune into the low voices drifting from other tents for an hour or so, along with some giggles and final trips to the toilet.

Stopping on my last toilet visit for the night, I looked up. The lack of light pollution meant the sky was crystal clear, the deepest and darkest black you can imagine, with a vast canopy of twinkling stars and an occasional shooting star whizzing across the expanse of space.

On that very existential note, I carefully picked my way back to the warmth of my sleeping bag and lay quietly mulling over the tales of Moroccan life that The Boss had told us as we sat around the small campfire before we all drifted off to bed.

Weary but content with their lot, most of our group were looking forward to the next day of trekking.

Funnily enough, I was physically exhausted, but my mind was buzzing, and I was worried about what the coming day might bring. To switch off and get some rest, I listened to my iPod for several hours before drifting off into a restless and uncomfortable sleep to the soothing strains of *Cafe del Mar* chill-out music.

I didn't get much more than three or four hours of sleep. My body craved some respite from the painkiller regime, so I let their effect wear off in the night and often the pain in my back brought me to fitful wakefulness in those long, cold, lonely hours when our fears come to the surface. Who knew what trials and tribulations we would face in the coming days?

CHAPTER NINE
Day Four – Auberge

Peering blearily through tired eyes, the luminous dial on my watch showed half past five. Not too early for me to be up and about.

The early hour gave me time to wake up slowly and prepare for the rigours of what promised to be our longest and most challenging day so far.

I was glad to get out of my sleeping bag. Although the bedrolls were quite thick, I could still feel the lumpy ground beneath, and my whole body ached.

Aware that my companions were still asleep, I eased myself stiffly upright. My back felt like a board and the rest of my body like a rag. Although there was still some residual numbness, I was manifestly relieved that the intense shooting pains in my thigh hadn't returned, thanks to my painkillers.

In the pitch blackness, the chilly air felt like a wet flannel against my skin as once again I faced the horrors of the toilet tent. With my torch held firmly between my teeth, I can't imagine what I must have looked like as I tried not to bring the flimsy structure down around my ears, holding onto the metal poles to haul myself upright. It was a close-run thing, and I couldn't resist a rueful chuckle. Even the pungent smell of our temporary toilet pit didn't spoil my rare moment of humour.

All sound travels long distances in the empty air as there is nothing else to compete. No cars, planes, barking dogs or machinery, just complete stillness and quiet. I could hear everything for miles around, and it was magic.

Soon enough, this serene start to the day was shattered by the cacophony of noise from awakening

148

desert dwellers, coughs, spits and sniffs, human and animal alike.

I could hear Chuckles doing her thing as her giggles floated in the still morning air and realised our cooks were already busy from the clatter of pots and pans echoing through camp. It was good to hear, and I relaxed a little as porters started to move around.

It wasn't long before everyone unzipped themselves from snug sleeping bags to prepare for our seven thirty departure.

Daylight came gradually, the sky lightening through shades of orange until the sun's rays started to blaze above the horizon, heralding swiftly rising temperatures.

With my bags already packed before breakfast, I took my time over pancakes smothered in jam and much-needed tea while chewing over the events of the previous day with some of my companions.

It was such a relief to discover that I was not the only one with health concerns as several of the others admitted to being less than fully fit, battling various aches and pains. However, I still kept the woeful state of my back to myself.

We were pushing ourselves beyond our normal limits, and something had to give. Some of my companions had blisters on blisters, and I really felt for them. The only way to reduce the discomfort was to lance and drain them, then strap the foot securely. The snaking queue outside Nia's tent grew longer as our bodies began to suffer. Many were doing the "Moroccan Mambo", our very own version of "Delhi Belly", so anti-diarrhoea pills were in great demand. I was glad I didn't have either problem; not yet anyway.

149

Regardless, spirits were high as The Boss and Bibi tried to chivvy us out of camp for an early start and our longest day of walking.

'Come on, everybody. Only half an hour left,' Bibi called. This was immediately followed by moans and groans of complaint from all directions.

'It's all very well,' I muttered to myself.

'What's the matter, Bossy One?' asked Sarah, looking up from her repacking.

'Oh, nothing much I suppose,' I replied wearily. 'Training all day on a Sunday was tiring enough. I just wasn't prepared for feeling so exhausted first thing in the morning.'

'I know what you mean,' butted in Steve, overhearing my grumbling. 'You usually have a week to recover but getting up and doing it all again day after day is tough. It's much harder than I expected. I don't know about you, but I'm worn out already.'

That was quite an admission from one of our hardiest trekkers. Steve was always at the front of the group and rarely complained.

Though we were tired and suffering from all manner of ailments, there was no question of any of us not continuing, but it would be a *very* long day.

We had camped in an area of flat, hard-packed sand, with a dune curving around behind us. We only had a few steps to go before we were into a large field of the infernal things.

'Thank goodness these are only low ones,' mumbled Sarah, plodding over the small ridges of windblown sand.

'It's a pity we can't skirt around them,' I said, feeling a bit ashamed at the thought. 'Mind you, it would spoil all the fun, wouldn't it?' I continued sarcastically. My mate rolled her eyes and laughed ruefully.

We both loved the dunes, but they did test our reserves of energy and resolve. Luckily, this particular morning they were not too challenging. Perhaps we were finally getting the hang of them.

As they petered out, we came across an abandoned Berber village with mudbrick buildings crumbling back into the desert sand.

While poking about amongst some of the derelict houses, my imagination was running riot. I could almost hear the laughter of children playing as their mothers, swaddled in layers of blue cotton, leaned against door frames chatting to their friends. Keeping one eye on their families, eyes sparkling, their giggles would erupt as they exchanged the latest village gossip. Perhaps the sun was beginning to get to me.

Our chatter left the echoing silence untouched. If those walls could only talk, we would have had a living history lesson.

It was good to have time to indulge in such visions, but practical matters took over during our early lunch stop.

We realised the ruins gave some privacy, so, once we'd finished eating, Sarah and I wandered off for the essential comfort stop. Being girls, we always went in pairs.

There we were, chatting about the day so far, exchanging snippets of news gleaned from our fellow trekkers, when the very worst possible thing happened to me.

I was squatting awkwardly when I felt a sharp dart of pain, and my back locked up completely. Finding it impossible to lever myself upright, I lost my balance and rolled forward into the soft sand.

'Oh no, help!' I yelled, knickers around my ankles, all semblance of dignity gone.

Sarah burst out laughing, with no thought for my composure. I couldn't blame her, as I must have made quite a sight with my ankles tangled in clothing, toilet paper in one hand, bum firmly in the air.

'Oh, my giddy aunt,' she gasped, absolutely beside herself. 'That's hilarious. Are you OK?' she finally managed to get out amidst the giggles.

'Do I bloody look OK?' I snapped, obviously not seeing the funny side of things. However, catching sight of my mate wiping away tears and trying not to snigger, I suddenly saw myself through her eyes and burst into fits of laughter as well as I lay there, immobilised in the sand, which was rapidly working its way into my important little places.

'Now, where's my camera when I need it?'

'Ooh, don't you dare. Give me a hand up you daft cow, before someone sees me.'

Looking up, my loss of dignity was complete. Some of the crew had stopped loading gear onto the truck and stood, chuckling and pointing in my direction.

Humiliated, I tried to amble nonchalantly back, painfully aware of the stifled laughter of the rest of the group. I think most people had a good laugh at my expense, although it was a while before I could relax enough to have a giggle with them.

As we hiked along a gully, the landscape quickly changed, and we ended up in the shadows between two outcrops of rock. The shade was very welcome, cooling us down, but it didn't last long. As we trudged on towards a ridge, we once again emerged into the full glare of the sun.

All around us the ground was covered in rocks of all sizes. Fortunately, a wide sandy track made the going a bit easier as we headed steeply upwards. Reaching the viewpoint at the top, we were now staring into a vast flat valley.

'Wow!' was all I could manage, eloquence lost in the sheer drama of the moment as the horizon merged with the haze in the far distance, with acres of clear blue sky overhead.

As I paused to take in the view, I felt rivulets of sticky sweat trickling down my back and began to notice the smell of my own body. The odour of fresh sweat wasn't altogether unpleasant, although I knew it would be a different story later on.

'Where do you think we'll get to tonight?' asked Sarah, seemingly a little overwhelmed by the vast expanse in front of us. I didn't have the heart to answer her because it seemed to go on forever.

The ground remained stony as we began to follow old Berber trails, winding onwards.

In some rare moments of respite, I found myself wondering about those ancient people who had gone before. Following their timeworn tracks was almost a privilege, imagining the thousands of weary feet that had made them over the years, clearing the stones aside as they walked.

How did they manage to survive in such a harsh environment? Did they find it as hard as we do? Speaking for myself, I think my life is soft in comparison. I complain about waiting in the supermarket queue, having driven there in my car; they had miles of trudging along narrow, dusty tracks to get anywhere. My lifestyle was a world away from theirs, and the realisation was humbling.

However, waxing lyrical was one thing, practicalities quite another. These trails were only the width of my boot, so I had to pay close attention.

Picking our way along the Berber trails.

Angela later commented that she noted how carefully I placed my feet on this part of the trek. I should say so. The stones were large enough to trip over or turn an ankle, so I found them especially troublesome.

I slowed down even further as my boots often slithered over rocks, jolting my back, making me catch my breath as pain shot down my leg. Even dulled by painkillers, it was still brutal enough to make me wince.

We had all come to rely on Nia and Angela to watch out for backmarkers, especially after comfort stops. It would have been a disaster to lose anyone. At least I got to chat with most of my companions as they dropped back to do the necessary and then inevitably carried on forwards, leaving me once again bringing up the rear.

Sarah was usually there with me too, with Bibi often carrying her daypack to reduce the load for her. It is amazing how much difference that can make when you are struggling to keep up. Carrying my bag slowed me down.

'I'm sorry to be such a slowcoach,' I apologised to Angela for the umpteenth time.

'Och no, don't worry yerself,' she replied in her soft Scottish brogue, not such a strong accent that I couldn't understand her, but a burr in her voice that was easy on the ears.

'You're not far behind, so it's OK. I am all for letting you know if it becomes a problem,' she reassured me. 'Anyway, it's a chance to get to know ye both a wee bit better.'

Feeling more positive about things, we trekked onwards, telling one another tall tales to keep our spirits up and while away the hours and the kilometres.

With my head down, concentrating on carefully placing my feet, I was grateful for Nia's company too, as she regaled me with stories of her adventures in some very remote places.

An intrepid and intelligent young woman, she was a real tonic, quick to relate a joke or funny anecdote, often at her own expense. I will never forget the yarns she had to tell.

In the moments alone with my thoughts, the desert crowded my senses. Dust and heat have their own strong, evocative effect. It's hard to describe, but you feel the intense rays of the sun burning into your body, combined with the taste of dust lingering in the air, swirled around by our footfalls.

I also noticed frequent scuttling sounds. Perhaps geckos, or other lizards, climbing between rocks to bask in the sun momentarily before hiding from its intense glare.

I had seen Scarab beetles on other trips and been fascinated by their antics as they busily rolled dung balls that far outweighed their tiny bodies. Perhaps they crawled across our paths, but I was so focused on sparing my back that I didn't notice much from my little bubble of concentration.

Snatches of conversation drifted back on the still air, growing fainter and more distant as I dropped further behind.

'You look pink, Sarah,' I mentioned later on, noticing she seemed puffed out. I didn't get a reply which told me all I needed to know, realising that the increasing heat was getting to her.

The going was slow, and the power of the sun relentless. It can get as hot as forty degrees (over one hundred Fahrenheit) in a Mallorcan summer, so I am used to it, although it does make me feel lethargic. Fortunately, the haze was keeping the temperature lower than that, so I wasn't feeling too bad, although I was hot and sweaty.

Slogging our way onwards, we couldn't wait for some signs that we were making progress. As the afternoon wore on, our shadows lengthened, and we were relieved to see the sun dropping towards the distant hills. Once it dipped behind them, we were able to breathe a sigh of relief as the temperature started to drop too.

However, the light was fading quickly, and we had no option but to keep pushing ourselves onwards as arriving after dark would have made it difficult to keep track of us all.

'Look, Trod, we're nearly there,' I exclaimed as a small oasis came into view. I could have cried with relief, realising this interminable day was almost over.

Sarah and I trudged on into camp, arriving just before dark. The walk had been long and rigorous, and I had found the last couple of hours boring, as the rocky terrain seemed never-ending.

'Oh, look, there's a camel.'

'Where?'

'Over there, you daft mare. He's reaching up into that thorn tree,' Sarah pointed out wearily. 'There must be a spring as there are a few palm trees scattered about.'

That camel eating his dinner at our oasis.

Looking around, I was surprised to see an *auberge* nearby, tucked into the lee of the red rock valley sides, its mudstone walls blending into the desert landscape. It struck me as bizarre to find such a monument to civilisation in a spot we had walked for days to find. There must have been roads, or at least tracks, nearby, but they were not obvious to our tired and gritty eyes.

'I can't wait to get this bag off my shoulders and relax. How about you, Trod?'

'Yeah, I'm absolutely worn out. How is your back holding up?'

Jo poked her head into our tent, interrupting our tired chatter and weary attempts to organise our bags.

'I don't suppose you're interested in a visit to the *auberge* before dinner?'

'Oh, yes,' I replied, without thinking, not wanting to miss out on anything. 'Is it far?'

'No, it's along that track at the back, maybe ten minutes from here.' 'Hmm, that'll be fifteen minutes lurching along for me then,' I thought. However, I was determined to join in, and most of our gang wanted to see if there was any ice-cold beer on offer, plus there were rumoured to be, wait for it, flushing toilets. It was enough to spur us into action.

'Come on, Trod, let's get sorted because the others are already leaving. I could murder a cold drink.'

'Me too,' she replied, stuffing the last of her toiletries into her backpack. 'Let's go. Have you got your torch?'

'Yes, and a hiking pole so I don't lose my footing in the dark.'

Looking back, I find it hard to believe we were so gung ho. The last thing either of us needed was more walking, along a rough track and in the dark. We were gluttons for punishment. However, the lure of a cold drink and flushing toilets, plus the thought that we might be missing out on something, was enough to get us moving.

It was probably only a ten-minute amble for the others, though it took us about twenty. However, it was worth it. The *auberge* was a welcome sight with softly lit mudbrick buildings surrounding a central courtyard and staff who seemed pleased to see us. A song popped straight into my head and stayed with me all evening. "Midnight at the Oasis" said it all.

Sadly, there were no beers, but we were offered a cool Coca Cola in the old-fashioned bottles. Delicious. It certainly qualified as one of the best cokes of my life as it trickled down my throat, washing away the desert dust.

It was a relief to sit in proper chairs and yarn a little, telling silly jokes and tall stories. We all made lots of visits to the flushing loos, bliss. They were still far from westernised; basic and, as always, smelly, but at least I could sit instead of squatting. I went three times, just to sit and ruminate on our adventures in relative privacy. Such are the highlights on a trip stripped bare of the luxuries we all take for granted.

We only stayed an hour or so, but it was a brief and welcome respite from the rigours of our trek. The Ibrahims knew the place and turned up for drinks too, chatting with the owners. Luckily, they had come in a truck, so Sarah and I had the added bonus of a lift back to camp.

Dinner was good with a substantial and tasty soup followed by couscous with vegetables and a little tender beef.

Someone was always complaining about the food, but I thought the crew did an excellent job of feeding us. After all, they were producing our meals from a tent. There were sixteen in our party, plus all the support crew, so they were catering for a large number of people and making sure we had sufficient fuel for our exertions.

Despite tucking in as if I hadn't eaten for a week, my trousers already felt loose on my waist.

After dinner, once again we gathered around a small campfire as the evening cooled down.

'Gosh, it's chilly, isn't it?' someone said. 'I'm off to fetch my fleece.'

'It is much colder,' I agreed. We were all feeling the noticeable drop in temperature.

'Look what we've got!' Toni and Becky danced out of their tent, waving a bag of some kind of treat over their heads. Nicnoc snatched it away to find marshmallows, ready to toast. What a delicious idea.

Fighting over the few sticks we could find, 'oohs' and 'aahs' of delight rang out, along with the occasional yelp as fingers and tongues got burnt. Black on the outside and runny in the middle, they were perfect.

It seems like a small thing, but somehow these moments stick in my mind, full of fun and a sense of togetherness. Only the twins kept themselves apart, preferring solitude with iPods firmly in place. It was their loss.

We were camped in the lee of the hills edging the immense flat valley, among some scrappy palm trees which were struggling to survive in the arid environment.

Peering out into the velvety blackness, a million stars twinkled overhead in the clear, unpolluted air of the desert night. With the only sounds our laughter, plus the occasional hawk and spit from the camels (and possibly their owners), it was easy to feel small and insignificant in the enormous emptiness.

I hadn't managed to appreciate such things very much so far as I was usually last into camp with little time to organise myself. It was good to stop and drink it all in, realising what a unique experience this was.

CHAPTER TEN
Day Five – Rock the Kasbah

'Wakey, wakey, Sarah. I've been up for ages.' I was keen to be up and moving.

Having woken around five o'clock, I was forced to lay still so as not to wake the others and had used the time to give myself a good talking to. Caught up with the pain from my back and worries about carrying a daypack, I had not been good company.

I had changed to a smaller backpack but decided it didn't seem fair to ask anyone to carry things for me, although Sarah was the guardian of our trail mix, and Nia generously carried my sarong in case I needed it. They can be used as extra protection from the sun or a screen whilst taking a pee. I wished I had used it the day before at my embarrassing lunch stop. I was mortified at the memory, and the incident was still causing some chuckles amongst our group. I don't think I'll be allowed to forget that.

Leaving early, it was still cool as we headed towards a dune field that appeared close but took us most of the day to reach. It was easy to misjudge distances when there were few points of reference.

Surprisingly, the morning was overcast, and we even had a few drops of rain. It wasn't enough to wet the ground properly, but it was the last thing we had expected in the Sahara.

However, it did make things easier. Without the glare of the white-hot desert shimmering in the distance, we could see things clearly, including the horizon.

We all picked up pace in the relative cool. I say relative, as it was still probably into the thirties (in the ninety-degree Fahrenheit range), much hotter than the norm for most of the others.

Thankfully, it felt cooler to me, and my back brace was much less sweaty than usual. I thanked my lucky stars that I had decided to wear it as it made a difference, holding my back firmly upright and supporting it through the jolts and bumps we encountered while walking over rough ground each day.

Not that any of this could be called normal. It was all extraordinary. I will always be able to visualise the scene of a vast hard-packed plain with the ant-like dots of trekkers making their way straight across it.

It was fairly easy going with no stones to avoid, no sinking and shifting sand to negotiate. Just an immense expanse of nothing which even overwhelmed the dunes in the distance.

A vast expanse of nothing.

Quite perversely, I loved the feeling of being dwarfed by the immensity of our surroundings. The massive arc of blue sky above was streaked with trails of thin grey cloud, veiling us from the full ferocity of the sun.

Once again, before we left, the medical tent had been inundated with people suffering various ailments. There weren't many of us who hadn't visited for some of Nia's particular brand of medical advice. Whatever was wrong, she would deal with it but had no patience with trying to guess the nature of a problem. There was absolutely no point in being coy.

She had been kept busy by the ever-increasing blister queue. I had never suffered from them before, so I didn't expect to now, as my boots were well worn in. I think everyone felt the same, and we were all surprised by how badly our feet held up.

Becky walked in flip flops all the way across the plain, her feet a mass of painful open wounds where the skin had lifted off. I admired her guts and determination to keep going.

I could hear some guffaws of laughter drifting back from those up front but couldn't quite make out what it was all about. Sarah put on a spurt to join the group and then dropped back to let me in on the joke.

'Oh, my goodness,' she giggled. 'We must have been sound asleep because the other girls' tent collapsed.'

'Do you mean in the middle of the night?'

'Yes,' she snorted, laughing again. 'You know the camels we saw when we came into camp? One of them wandered across and knocked over one of their supporting poles.'

'Oh my God, I would have had a hissy fit,' I exclaimed. 'I can't believe we didn't hear anything. That lot would have been laughing fit to burst.'

'Or squealing with fright more like.'

163

'Yes,' I replied. 'If the canvas had dropped on top of me, I would've yelled my head off. Everyone would have known about it.'

'Apparently, it was only the front corner, so it didn't fall on anyone, but the whole tent sagged down really low. I think they only found what had happened for sure when they woke up this morning. What a laugh,' chuckled Sarah, wiping her eyes and enjoying the image conjured up in her imagination. I'm sure it would have been a different story if the camel had come in our direction.

Once again, there was no shelter whatsoever as we carried on. Frequent short breaks allowed people to catch up again after a comfort stop. It was important that we didn't become too strung out, so those brief halts allowed me to join up with the middle of the pack. Some of our group were once again doing the "Moroccan Mambo". I will leave that to your imagination…

We must have looked a motley crew, inching our way across that wilderness. While I have long believed in covering up in the heat in lightweight clothing, it made a change to wear shorts occasionally although some people were still wearing them all the time, despite the constant warnings from Angela about the dangers of too much exposure to the sun. The Moroccan crew were shielded from head to toe, with colourful scarves wound around head and neck. They were essential whenever the wind whipped up the sand, preventing it from blowing into eyes, ears and mouth.

'Come on, Trod,' I nagged.

'OK, OK,' came the chirpy reply. 'Let's get on with it. Are we really going to walk right across that?'

164

'I'm not sure. It's just as well The Boss knows where we're going.' With that, we set out across the most enormous expanse I have ever seen.

The horizon shimmered in the far distance as we fell into small groups, determined to complete yet another long, tough day.

Getting into a rhythm, using my poles alternately to push me along, I found I had enough energy to chat to whoever chose to drop back and join me in my usual spot, bringing up the rear.

At times Sarah forged ahead, chatting with others, before falling back to plod wearily along next to me.

'I can't believe you push yourself so hard with your health issues,' I said to Des, our elder statesman.

'You've got to keep challenging yourself, haven't you? Or else you're better off dead.' That was his philosophy for life, and I could identify with that.

Des turned out to be one of the fastest walkers with an extensive store of accumulated knowledge on many subjects, which sometimes brought him in for some light-hearted ribbing from certain members of our party. Thankfully, he took it all in good spirits.

'Can anyone see those wee specks in the distance?' asked Angela at our first rest stop. Occupied with untangling water tubes, reapplying the necessary sunscreen or nibbling energy-giving snacks, none of us took too much notice.

'Look,' she insisted. 'It's a camel train, and we'll cross paths in the next half-hour or so.'

Abandoning all other activities, we stared into the shimmering haze and could make out the thin moving line. How exciting and exotic.

'No one is to ask for a ride, though,' added Angela, puncturing any plans we were starting to make.

'Why not?' demanded one of the twins.

'Company policy I'm afraid. A wee lass fell off one of the blasted creatures a couple of years ago and broke her arm, so we're no insured for such adventures, sadly,' she explained.

This caused a few moans and groans, along the lines of 'Bloomin' 'elf and safety. They spoil all our fun.'

Dragging daypacks back on, we tramped further into the void, a certain jauntiness in our step, excited at the prospect of meeting a *caravanserai*.

That camel is definitely smirking.

It came into focus as our two lines merged until we stood in the centre of this vast nothingness with half a dozen Berber traders leading their pack animals.

I am not a big fan of camels, having had dealings with these smelly, obstreperous "ships of the desert" before, so I gave them a wide berth. Bibi, once again, became our David Bailey as numerous cameras were produced for photos, the infernal animals smirking in the background.

Something about it felt staged. That we had managed to cross paths at all was almost unbelievable, but these were genuine merchants, on their way to market.

We were all buzzing from our encounter. There was a spring in our step as we got back into our stride.

'How are we doing, Trod?' I asked for the umpteenth time. I probably drove my mate ever so slightly mad with that question.

'OK, ta. Thanks for asking,' she replied, but the slight quiver in Sarah's voice told me she was struggling.

I tried to relax a little in the knowledge that the overcast skies were protecting us from the full ferocity of the sun.

'I can't believe we've covered that whole plain,' I exclaimed later over lunch. Several voices chimed in, agreeing that the morning and the kilometres had passed quickly.

'Hey, Trod, more dunes this afternoon.'

'I know. We're almost in them already,' she replied, sounding tense.

Despite feeling more relaxed about our capabilities, we were still a bit apprehensive about crossing more of them.

'Don't worry, we'll manage. Aren't they an amazing sight? We might get to race down a few today or, even better, some dune rolling.'

I was trying to be upbeat, catching onto the general mood of excitement amongst the group. However, I was worried about the upcoming challenge. Struggling onwards, heaving and pushing with my poles was becoming second nature, but racing down them was an entirely different proposition.

I would have loved to slide straight down like a kid on a tin tray, but it just wasn't going to be happening for me. I would be favouring my back, gingerly inching down sideways.

I had only confided in Sarah and wasn't about to let on to anyone else how it felt to take things so carefully. They probably thought I was a proper party pooper.

Puffing and sweating after slogging our way up, we gathered at the top of the steepest ridge. The view was fantastic. We were overlooking a sea of dunes. Waves of them stretched in every direction, all the way to the distant horizon.

They had been blown into row after row of enormous curves, with dark shadows in the wind-carved hollows and starkly exposed ridges in the full glare of the sun.

There was little else to catch the eye, other than some scrappy clumps of sharp leafed grasses and a few stunted trees growing out of the sand.

After much debate, several people held hands to run at full tilt, screaming and laughing on their way down, some rolling and ending up in a big heap in the soft sand at the bottom.

Dusting themselves off, they stood, encouraging the rest of us to take the plunge. Eventually, Sarah was coaxed into a headlong run which left her breathless and red-faced. Feeling very left out, I hung back, realising Angela and Nia were still waiting at the top to make sure everyone got down safely.

'Oh, go on, I'll be fine,' I said, hoping they would wait a little further on for me to catch up. Taking me at my word, they raced noisily downhill together. While they were busy talking to my mate, I took my time and, unobserved, inched my way painfully down

A sea of sand dunes.

To say I felt fed up was an understatement, but I had rolled down a dune before, and I knew how exhilarating it could be. I just wanted to do it again.

Taking a quick break for a drink, I mentally pulled myself up by my bootstraps and carried on, trying not to fall too far behind.

Later, whilst eating lunch, I found sitting on the carpeted ground almost impossible and spent most of our rest break ambling gently around to keep my aching body on the move.

We ate a hot and tasty vegetable tagine with lots of freshly made flatbread. It was good and wholesome and would keep us going until dinner.

Near our lunch stop was a mudbrick walled *kasbah*. The small fortress looked deserted as if it was crumbling back into its surroundings, blending into the pale terracotta of the desert. There was not one intact wall, and the former gardens were scruffy and overwhelmed with sand with just a forlorn rose bush or two surviving.

'Word is there are toilets and cold drinks over there,' blurted Sarah, hurrying over to me. 'Are you up for it? It's only a few minutes' walk on the flat.'

'Really?' I asked, disbelieving her every word.

'Well, I reckon it's worth investigating,' she huffed, so off we went, the thought of a loo and cold Coca Cola egging us onwards.

'It looks abandoned if you ask me. It obviously was a fine building once, but how could anyone live there now?' I grumbled, at which point Angela caught up to us with reassurances that the extra effort would be worthwhile.

'We go around the side, through the blue doorway and into the courtyard. There are some squat toilets but better than *au natural* I reckon,' she added cheerfully.

Sure enough, both things were available. The cokes were lukewarm, but the loos were bearable, and I managed not to wee on my boots this time. It's a big problem of mine when going bush, and my suede leather boots told their own story.

A few minutes later, Sarah and I were contemplating our return to the shade of our rest stop. We had only seen the merest peek of a headscarved Berber lady whose giggles we could hear as we gave The Boss (who had suddenly popped up at the *kasbah*) our few *dirhams* in payment for the Coca Cola.

Thankfully, he had the jeep with him, so we got a lift back, only to find some of our companions looking at local jewellery. Once again, a market stall had suddenly appeared right in front of our lunch tent where a couple of local teenage girls showed their entrepreneurial talents, having brought a blanket full of trinkets they had made and hoped that we would buy.

I had found enough space to stretch out full length in the shade and wasn't about to move for any possible enticement.

'Did you get anything?' I asked Sarah who had gone to look.

'No, there isn't much worth having. The girls were more interested in getting us to give them things as souvenirs,' she explained. 'You were right to stay and rest. I wish I had too. Still, we've got another half an hour yet. Can I lie down next to you?'

The next thing we knew, hands were clapping next to our ears.

'Come on, you two. It's time to go.' Angela had spotted that we were quietly dozing in the corner, but it was time to get moving again.

We trudged directly back into the dunes. Fortunately, the sky remained overcast, keeping the temperature bearable, but hats were still essential, plus lashings of lotion on sunburned legs and faces.

Sarah was once again struggling. Her short legs kept sinking into the soft, shifting sand, and the frequent comfort stops for her upset stomach were not helping matters. It did, however, give me a bit of breathing space, allowing me to slog on.

Silently, with teeth gritted and pushing my poles into the slope ahead of me, I hauled myself upwards while listening to the laughs and cheers of the rest as they held hands and hared speedily down. Meanwhile, I plodded slowly on towards the summit.

As a reward for getting ourselves up the first steep, majestic crescent of the afternoon, a wide expanse of desert stretched out in front of us.

'That's amazing!' I exclaimed to Nia, who was keeping me company.

'Do you know, I have to agree with you, even though I've seen lots of views like this. It's a truly awesome sight,' she replied.

It was all I could do to keep going, edging carefully sideways on the downward slopes. I used my frequent breaks to concentrate on the awe-inspiring views, which were all I had ever hoped they would be, with dunes stretching out in every direction to the horizon.

Edging along the ridges, ever higher, we resembled ants on the march. The Boss led us into the centre of the field, aiming for the highest point, which would make that morning's feat seem quite tame in comparison.

That afternoon, my companions threw themselves into the ultimate experience of galloping over the summits whooping and hollering, some tripping and rolling, packs filling with sand, laughing as they raced one another down.

Most people had carried on by the time I reached the bottom, feeling a little glum and lonely, standing still to ease out the increasing pains in my back and the tingling in my left leg.

'Are you OK, Dawne?' asked Nia, looking at me with some concern.

'Oh, yes,' I blustered. 'Just regrouping. So, tell me about your last adventure,' I asked, hoping to change the subject.

'Let's get going again, and I might be tempted to tell you about it.'

Pushing myself forwards, I rolled on, looking for all the world like a drunken sailor. I needed to gain momentum for the next dunes, which, thankfully, became smaller as the day progressed.

I breathed a sigh of relief as we finally negotiated our way out to find ourselves once again on hard-packed ground at the edge of the plain.

Skirting around the edge of other sandhills, it began to spit with rain. Yes, it was determined to rain on us in this desert. It shouldn't happen, should it? The sky looked grey and stormy, but we only had occasional spits and spots as we carried onwards.

Walking through an area of grassy hummocks, Bibi suddenly stopped by a circle of wood on the ground, covering a hole with a wall of bricks surrounding it, only some six inches or so high.

'You look, you look,' he urged. 'Is water.' As we crowded around, sure enough, he lowered a bucket a few feet to bring up to the surface fresh, clear and cold water, overflowing onto our hands and faces as he tipped it forwards.

He explained that wherever you find hard-packed sand with grassy hummocks, you will find underground aquifers. What a surprise.

There is so much to learn about survival in the desert, and the ancient ways can help us understand the environment. I was fascinated by it all. Certainly, hints on how to find water in such arid terrain could be a lifesaver.

The rest of the day turned out to be a hard slog. The Boss didn't seem sure where the camp was set up and sent several of his team out to scout the area.

'Oh my God, we haven't got to go up there, have we?' exclaimed Sarah, pointing to the guys who had just run up a huge, high dune.

'Och no, don't panic,' chuckled Angela. 'The walkie-talkie battery has died, so they've gone up to try and spot the camp.' It was a good job they knew the area as I didn't fancy being out there all night.

Finding water in the desert.

We plodded on and on through another dune field, avoiding the largest ones but still struggling through soft, shifting sands.

It wasn't too hot, but Sarah was exhausted. With this long day coming on top of her awful start to the trip, Bibi was helping out by carrying her daypack.

We just had to carry on, heads down. Most of our other companions were well on their way, while I was gossiping with first Nia and then Angela and sometimes The Boss, busy concentrating on putting one foot in front of the other while half-listening to their traveller's tales.

The Boss was a fount of knowledge about the area and kept us interested with stories of other treks and telling me about his family in the High Atlas Mountains.

'Are we nearly there yet?' I asked Angela, loath to admit that I was absolutely shattered. I wanted camp to appear *now*. I wasn't alone as everyone was weary from the very long day.

Last in as usual, Sarah and I approached the tents in near darkness, the faint twilight suddenly switching into velvety blackness as we gratefully sank onto chairs and drank the proffered glasses of Moroccan sweet mint tea.

Rifling through my bag and gathering up bits and pieces, I suddenly turned to her.

'Oh no, I can't believe it, my hat has gone. I must have dropped it as we came into camp. It's a disaster!' I wailed, almost in tears of frustration and exhaustion. 'I can't believe I lost my hat.' All my fears came rushing in as I tried not to weep and wail over such a trifle.

'Hey, don't worry, Bossy One. I'm sure it will turn up,' Sarah reassured me, probably wondering why I was such a wuss.

'Why did I ever think I could do this?' I cried. 'A knock-kneed knackered old baggage like me.'

I wish I could say I am a rufty-tufty person, but I am just a middle-aged woman, struggling with the physical effects of ageing, finding myself in an unlikely environment, scrabbling to keep pace rather than show myself up.

Above all, I was acutely aware of not wanting to let down all those people who had believed in me enough to donate to Thrombosis UK, all because I said I could complete this challenge.

Finish it I would, but I was feeling properly sorry for myself. Poor Sarah, having to deal with my angst while she was pushing herself beyond her usual limits. She was the heroine of the hour as far as I was concerned.

My ever-patient friend needed a wash down (wet wipes for me), so I went along to hold her clothes and fight off our imaginary demons in the dark, all the while chuntering away to myself.

'Get on with it. You can do this. You're fine, with or without your blasted hat. Lighten up.'

Meanwhile, we were all tired and aching from such a long day's slog. There was one bit of good news. My boots had stayed glued together. What a great relief that was.

The next day would be hard, coming hot on the heels of our exertions today. By half past eight, some very tired trekkers once again crawled off into the comfort of our sleeping bags.

Sadly, it was not to be a good night's sleep as the wind picked up, and all we could hear was the sound of it whistling eerily across the plain, curling into camp like a snake, rattling guy ropes and any loose flaps of canvas. At times, it sounded like the Hounds of Hell were at our door.

I put my head into the hood of my sleeping bag and closed my eyes, hoping for the relief of deep and healing sleep. Sadly, it wasn't to be.

Despite feeling thoroughly exhausted, I felt increasing pain as the daily dose of painkillers began to wear off. Deeply uncomfortable, it was all I could do to lay quietly and listen to the mayhem outside until it was time to get up and do it all over again.

CHAPTER ELEVEN
Day Six – Our Last Day

'It's our last day. I'm not sure how I feel about that,' said Sarah over breakfast.

We were all feeling weary with the accumulated effort of the week plus a poor night's rest because of the wind howling like a banshee.

'What a shame we didn't get to sleep out on the dunes last night.' I had looked forward to that possibility since it was suggested earlier in the week.

'Oh, I don't know. I reckon you would have been awake all night, fretting about bugs getting inside your sleeping bag.'

'You're probably right. I just liked the idea of it, like staying out in the garden all night when we were kids, and it would have been a real desert experience.'

I wished we could have counted the myriad stars that twinkle on most clear evenings out there. However, cloud and squalls put paid to the plan.

Though not much actual rain fell, it had sounded like someone throwing a handful of small stones against our tents. The wind was persistent, working its way around and into any gaps in our carefully constructed shelters. Old canvas, laced together around wooden poles, hadn't kept much of anything out.

It was another overcast day, but there was a feeling of anticipation in the air as we packed for the last time. Our bags were hard to close, disorganised by now and full of dirty laundry. There was probably a kilo or two of sand in them by then too.

'Here it is, I found it,' Bibi called, walking into the camp from the surrounding dunes, gaily waving my sunhat around his head.

'You wonderful man,' I exclaimed, reaching up to retrieve the precious object.

Bibi smiled broadly, acknowledging the short round of applause from our breakfast companions.

'I'm so happy to get it back,' I cried, in reply to Sarah's look of amusement. 'Sorry I was such a grump about it last night. It just seemed like the last straw. I guess it was a bit of an over-reaction,' I added, by way of apology, receiving a heartfelt hug from my pal. I was a happy person that morning.

I dutifully swallowed the obligatory painkillers and pulled my back brace firmly into place. Bags packed, we were ready to go except that, for the first time, I had to join the forlorn queue outside Nia's tent.

'Hi, Dawne. What can I do for you?'

'I'm a bit embarrassed, as I was boasting about never having blisters, and now I've got one.' It hadn't been much of a plan to ignore the start of it yesterday, hoping it wouldn't fill up with too much fluid. I seemed to have others underneath the sole of my foot, deep inside, but they would have to sort themselves out.

'Yeah, this one needs attention, Dawne. Even I've got a couple this trip which is most unusual. It's been a toughie. Are you comfortable while I drain it?' Nia had noticed I was half laid down, unable to sit up properly whilst on the ground.

'Oh, I'll survive,' I muttered, not wanting a discussion. I was far from relaxed, but it just wasn't possible to bend my body forwards, so I pretended to be lounging rather than trying to sit.

Frustratingly, once the blister was popped, drained and taped, I had to lie there while my boot was re-strapped onto my foot. Gaffer tape was once again the hero of the hour. The glue was fine, but we had given our

178

footwear a fair bashing in the last day or two. The tape was "belt and braces" to ensure I could carry on without a problem.

Did I feel humiliated? Yes. There was no choice other than to bluff my way through with a giggle, and some comment about being waited on hand and foot. Thank goodness Nia had a wonderful sense of humour.

'What time do you call this?' I joked to Angela. 'Eight o'clock? That's almost a lie in. Are we only doing half a day then?'

That got everyone chuckling as we donned our daypacks and set out across a plain of hard-packed but stony sand, interspersed with thorn trees and the occasional grassy hummock.

Everyone seemed to have slowed down so that, for the first time, Sarah and I found ourselves in the centre of the group. Some people were hanging back, needing to make use of any sparse vegetation to duck behind.

Des looked to have aged ten years that morning, suffering from a very upset stomach, as were most of my companions. For once, I was grateful for my almost OCD obsession with washing my hands, using sanitiser and not eating anything uncooked or unpeeled. At this point, I think frequent squats in the bushes would have finished me off.

The accumulation of effort over the last few days was taking its toll. Painkillers were becoming less and less effective, and the pain in my back intensified, but I had been warned. 'Do not be afraid of the pain.' Those words from my doctor haunted me, but at least I knew what was going on.

Once I was up and into my own particular rhythm of walking, things began to improve. I was on a roll ("What shall we do with the drunken sailor" once again sprang to mind), keeping up the momentum. Stops were the hard part. Sitting down on the ground was impossible, and I spent most of our breaks wandering slowly around. The only alternative was to lie down.

Fortunately, the agonising shooting pains I had experienced before the trek had not returned. They would have stopped me in my tracks as I would have been unable to put my left foot to the ground. However, onwards…

Stiff, deeply weary and in pain, I was still battling through and determined to enjoy the last few hours of our adventure.

'How are you feeling, Bossy One? Will you stand guard for me behind this tree? I need to stop again.' Sarah's stomach was all over the place and she was beginning to despair of the many comfort stops.

'I'm OK, thanks. I don't need a loo break, but here's a good spot,' I said, gesturing towards a sheltered hummock of grass that might do a better job than the slender tree she was aiming for.

'Give me your pack,' I suggested, holding it up to keep the water tube from falling into the sand. There's nothing worse than gritty slurps of water for the rest of the day. I wasn't about to let on about how I felt, so it seemed better to focus on my friend and her needs.

At that point, the effort required to keep going was overwhelming, moving one walking pole in front of the other, watching for any stones which might cause me to stumble. Anything that jolted my back sent a bolt of lightning pain through my entire body.

My trousers were hanging on my hips, and I could step out of them without undoing the zip. They were snug at the start, but now I was grateful for the belt of my bum bag to hold them up. It was a hell of a way to lose weight.

Heading towards a line of trees, shimmering in the heat as we set out, I was surprised that the mirage effect still happened, even on such an overcast day. Cloudy it may have been, but the sun appeared periodically, and it was still hot by most people's standards.

It had all changed by the time we arrived at our lunch stop. It was raining with a light mist obscuring our view of the tops of the surrounding hills. What we could see of them made it look as if they were eroding into multicoloured hillocks caused by the minerals exposed as they crumbled back into the desert.

The whole afternoon was dull and overcast with intermittent rain showers, none enough to soak us, but we needed our light showerproof jackets.

'I knew there would be a use for these,' laughed Sarah. We had considered leaving them at home, thinking they would be the last thing we would need in the Sahara. We wore them most of that afternoon, alternately sweaty and chilly.

Crashed out under the thorn trees, we made a subdued group, perhaps contemplating the achievement of a goal that had enthralled each of us for some months past.

I could hear a few giggles as our pal Woody was photographed in several compromising positions. Yes, Woody from *Toy Story* had made another appearance. His bemused grin had made its way into lots of our pictures. Glancing around me, I thought that we looked like a right bunch of characters, never mind our mascots. 'Into infinity and beyond...'

We had a relaxed walk that final afternoon, passing through a Berber village where we were accosted by bunches of ragged kids with their hands outstretched to grasp whatever trinkets we had thought to bring.

'Gift, gift,' they called, dirty brown faces split by grins designed to charm and beguile us.

They must have learned the word from passing hikers. Often trek instructions ask you not to bring sweets and give pens and paper to local children, but the girls had some marshmallows left and wanted to give them away.

Of course, as soon as a couple of kids gathered, more appeared as if by magic. Toni soon had a cluster of them, barging about, desperate to see what she had on offer. Her schoolteacher instincts came to the fore as she shouted at them not to push and to please 'Form an orderly queue,' which left us all in fits of laughter. That was just not going to happen.

A few brightly dressed but fully covered Berber women came out to watch our motley crew pass by. It seemed strange to see mudbrick and sand homes with large satellite dishes outside. Yes, really. They must have had generators to supply electricity. I did peer at some old, obviously working machinery, which might have done the trick.

I would love to have seen inside one of the houses. The mixture of traditional and modern must be quite something.

Women were shyly peeking around doorways, dressed in colourful robes and scarves, looking excitedly at whatever their kids were showing them in outstretched hands.

Waving at us, the children were bolder, following us for some time, always at a safe distance but happy to be photographed if we asked nicely.

Berber women, gossiping outside their homes.

'Oh, look, Trod. Rabbits.' Peering over the rim of a circular stone pen, we found a collection of cute bunnies, evidently not pets but dinner, which I pointed out to her disgust.

There were big heaps of branches stacked outside these homes, gathered for fires used for cooking, and to keep them warm during the cold winter nights. They were a precious resource as trees were few and far between.

Some of the houses were painted in blue or white with traditional Berber symbols on the walls.

Families had come down to the plains now that the snows had reached the High Atlas. They would take their goats and camels back when the intolerable summer heat returned.

It was interesting and relaxed walking, each of us joining up in clusters to talk over our experiences, only to separate and take time for private thoughts. This was the end of a journey that had taken most of us many months to complete, often life-changing, and it took some processing.

It was a short day with camp coming into view in the late afternoon. We were still all bunched together, and someone called out.

'Let's walk together. Come on, hold hands, and we can all finish at the same time.'

Even I was there. Looking around me at our somewhat weather-beaten and grubby crew, I felt a rush of camaraderie and could see a range of emotions drawn on each face.

It was a more powerful moment than I could ever have expected, and tears gathered in the dust at the corners of my eyes, despite my best efforts to hold them at bay.

As we gathered in the centre of our camp, many of us began unashamedly crying and hugging those closest to us. Unwilling to give in at first, it eventually overwhelmed both me and Sarah. She who *never* cries.

Our biggest hugs were reserved for one another, but the emotions kept on coming for all of us, the men included. I think each of us was thinking about our reason for doing this trek. We may have lost someone to the cause we were supporting or have experienced the rigours of the disease involved, such as cancer or, in my case, blood clots. Many of us were lucky to be alive.

It was a double-edged sword for me. I was happy to have survived my thrombosis ordeal but had lost my dad to a blood clot, and he was uppermost in my mind at that point.

Photos were duly taken, and tears wiped away. I took time to talk with both Nia and Angela, to thank them in the most heartfelt fashion for their help and support. I

The final group photo.

chose this time to tell them about the troubles with my back, which brought the emotion of it all back again.

'Och, no, don't get upset, Dawne.'

'I'm just so relieved I managed it,' I cried, voice wobbling. 'I couldn't have done it without you. Please don't think badly of me for not telling you in advance.'

'Ye've done well. Even more so than I realised, Dawne. You're a sensible lass, and you know your limits. All credit to you. What an achievement.'

'Oh, I can't stop crying. Don't mind me. Didn't you ever wonder why I was struggling with the walking?'

'I only noticed a couple of days ago when you were picking your way very carefully through the stones on those narrow Berber trails. I understand now, but I never thought you were particularly troubled.'

'At the back of the line as usual,' piped up Nia. 'I thought you just enjoyed our company,' she joked.

'Well, I can't thank both of you enough for all your support.' These heartfelt words were only lightened when I pulled up my t-shirt to show them my soaking wet back brace.

'I'm glad we didn't know about that. It's truly disgusting, and it's dripping with sweat. Yuk.' With that, they both wandered off to congratulate other members of the assembled company. Often words were unnecessary. Sometimes a hug says it all.

Both Nia and Angela were generous and kind in their comments, and it took me some time to get the pent-up feelings out of my system.

The relief we all felt, plus a little sadness for the end of something important, brought us together for a fun-filled and hilarious evening. Tired we undoubtedly were, but a fresh boost of adrenalin pushed us to make the most of our last night in the desert.

We ate a hearty meal of vegetable tagine with chunks of some kind of meat and lingered over mint tea and biscuits, crowding ever closer to the campfire as the night became the coldest we had yet encountered.

The Boss told us there was snow on the mountains now. Each of us crept away at some point to put on a fleece and socks, before moving our chairs into the welcome circle of warmth. No early night tonight. It was party time, Berber style.

Amidst much giggling and a certain air of shyness, the porters, cooks and crew gathered around, holding an assortment of plastic bowls, water containers, a drum, tin tray, and one plastic jerry can. We realised this was the band, and for the next half an hour we were treated to traditional Berber songs to the accompaniment beaten out on these makeshift instruments. It was brilliant.

Faces shining in the firelight, white teeth flashing in the dark, they brought us their culture, unexplained but vibrant beats, these men stamping their way forwards and backwards in a higgledy-piggledy line.

At one point, several jeeps arrived, beeping horns breaking the solitude of our camp. Their passengers were curious about the noise and hilarity. Unsure what to make of us, a few men in traditional full-length *djellabas* joined in the clapping and shuffling, putting to rest our fears that they may have had less amusing intentions. Eventually, they headed off back into the velvety darkness.

Entertainment, Berber style.

This was not a night for staring at the canopy of stars sparkling like diamonds in the desert night, more a time of laughter and celebration. Contemplation would come in the quiet of the early hours, snuggled up in our sleeping bags.

The Berber men were full of giggles, just like the women. During our time in camp, we could hear the only female on the team, our cook I had nicknamed Chuckles. We did not see her until our final morning, but her laughter, interspersed with the clanging of cooking pots, rang out every morning and evening. The men were just as bad, and it was infectious.

Tired, happy faces smiled out of the gloom as we clapped along, trying to join in, much to their amusement.

Our turn came to reciprocate with some English songs, but we made a pretty poor show. Nia shone, singing us a traditional Welsh tune but the rest of us only managed random verses from pop songs, even attempting the torch-lit shot of Queen singing "Bohemian Rhapsody", until we forgot the words.

By ten o'clock we were all feeling the rigours of our late night. Well, it was late compared to all our other nights out in the desert. We had already lost some of our team who had crashed out even while the campfire was still burning.

Some moments will stick in my mind from that evening. Principally Steve who announced we should sing "It's my party" to which the first line is "Nobody knows where my Johnny has gone". The assembled company dissolved into fits of hysterical laughter, one of those moments when I guess you had to be there.

Before long, we were tucked up snugly, although I'm not sure how many of us slept due to the high winds, frequent rain showers, plus thunder and lightning. It was an uncomfortable night as flashes illuminated our flapping tent openings while rain crept through the gaps and started to soak through the old-fashioned canvas. It's just as well everything dries out quickly in the desert heat.

CHAPTER TWELVE
Day Seven – Return to Ouarzazate

'Hey, Trod, look, beautiful blue skies.' Sarah shielded her eyes as I lifted aside the wet tent flaps to let the sunshine in. Drops of rain, shining like diamonds, rolled off the canvas and disappeared into the thirsty desert sands.

'You're crying again?'

'Oh, don't mind me,' replied my pink-eyed friend. 'Look what you've done,' she grumbled. 'I never cry.'

'I knew it would be my fault,' I blustered back, feeling weepy too. The accumulated fears and worries, plus the grit and determination expended on completing this trek, were taking their toll.

With such a shocking introduction to the desert, I think that Sarah willed herself to get through it. My emotions centred more on feeling overwhelming relief at having come through this experience without a major drama over the problems with my back.

Once again, I wandered over to Angela and Nia to reiterate how much I appreciated their company and support over the past few taxing days. Of course, that made me shed a few more tears.

Our final breakfast was more leisurely than usual, the sense of achievement and camaraderie remaining strong among the group. Nostalgia and recollections would wait for this evening, but we had to get through the jeep trip first after more 'thank yous' and heartfelt goodbyes to the Moroccan ground crew, including Chuckles, our giggling cook.

It was the first time we had met her, lined up with the rest of the team. Introduced by The Boss, they were strangely shy at being in the spotlight, our applause and cheers making some of them squirm in embarrassment. It was our way of expressing gratitude for their positive and friendly attitude. It had added much to our experience. Their solving some of our problems helped too, principally fixing my boots. Thanks, guys.

'They look a bit overwhelmed don't you think?'

'Strangely, they do,' replied Sarah. 'You'd think they would be used to this after every trek, wouldn't you?' Angela, right next to us, laughed and agreed.

'Perhaps you lot wore them out last night. We had quite an evening, didn't we?'

'Isn't it always like that?' I queried.

'Och, no. It depends on the group. Sometimes people can be less than appreciative of their efforts. You lot haven't complained about anything, and that sticks in their minds.'

'Are you all ready?' called Angela, clapping her hands, and rounding up the stragglers to herd us back into the jeeps.

'It's already eight o'clock, and we've got a long drive back to Ouarzazate. Remember, we want to have enough time for you all to make a wee visit to the *hammam*. We've our last night celebration too.'

'I've always wanted to go to one of these bathhouses. At least it will get us good and clean again. I'm filthy,' laughed Sarah.

'Oh no,' I groaned. 'There's no way I'm going to let any stranger loose on my back. I might give that a miss.' At that point, I would rather have stuck pins in my eyes than allow anyone to rub, pummel or even wash my poor battered body. It was far from my idea of relaxation.

Shoehorning ourselves back into the dusty jeeps, we felt like intrepid adventurers returning from the wilds. However, tiredness overwhelmed our little band, despite the same chaotic driver from the trip out. No one objected to my quiet request for the front seat, so Sarah, Jo and Polina were once again jolted around in the back, despite which they were soon fast asleep.

The journey seemed long but not as interminable as the outbound one, and we knew that we were on our way to a reasonable hotel for a fun-filled evening before flying home the next day. More importantly, flushing toilets and hot showers awaited our filthy bodies, itching from desert dust and hair like Brillo pads, stiff with sand.

Determinedly strap hanging once again, I cast my mind back; smiles at the funny moments, a squirm or two over embarrassing incidents, and sheer relief at having achieved our goal. A couple of quick truck stops helped ease the stiffness in my back, but not for long. I wanted the jolting to end as I daydreamed of a soft bed and a hot shower.

Once phone signals were back, I sent several cheerful messages to interested parties. My mum was very relieved to hear from me and so proud of my achievement. Her simple and heartfelt words brought tears to my eyes yet again. I had kept the true extent of my back troubles from her.

Only Bernie knew of the dark hours of doubt I had experienced in the weeks leading up to our departure and could fully appreciate how I felt. No doubt he was glad it was over too, as I had put him through quite an ordeal. His texted reply was full of congratulations and joy, plus details of our meeting that evening.

He had decided to fly over and meet us all in Ouarzazate, and I couldn't wait for a massive hug. Everyone knew he was going to be there, and were eager to meet him, Sarah in particular as he was our supporter.

Mulling things over to myself, I couldn't take my eyes off the scenery flashing by. My pals were asleep and the driver busy, so I couldn't share my fascination with the distant snow caps of the High Atlas Mountains, glinting in the sun.

We were belting along good roads on a flat plain with this awesome sight in the background. No wonder our nights had become extremely chilly as the week went on. On our arrival, there had been no snow. Falls had been quite heavy in the past few days.

We had been sheltered from the tourist traps of Morocco until now, but on the way back we stopped at the ubiquitous carpet factory. Piling out of the jeep, I was glad of the rest and chance to stretch my legs, ambling down back lanes with mudbrick houses on either side until we reached our destination.

'I don't know why we have to stop here,' I grumbled.

'No, me neither. None of us will buy a carpet, will we?' muttered Trod.

Having said that, we were greeted warmly and plied with sweet mint tea as we watched a demonstration of weaving given by a local woman. She was swathed in blue cotton with strange tribal markings on her face, and I was mesmerised by her shining brown eyes, which danced with laughter.

It proved to be interesting and informative, sat in a small room amongst some of the most beautiful rugs I have ever seen. However, we were the wrong crowd to try and sell to. Our sights were set firmly on hot showers, soft beds and flushing toilets.

At our second stop, I had to rouse Sarah and her sleeping companions. We were in the Dades Valley where roses grow in abundance, and there was a shop selling all things rose-scented.

'Come on, Trod, it's lunchtime. I've got your packed lunch.'

'I hope there are no boiled eggs this time,' she grumbled, not wanting a repeat of the sickness she had suffered at the start of our adventure.

'I'm not that hungry really, just shattered,' she continued.

'Are you thirsty then?' I asked, offering her my water bottle, knowing there could be cold Coca Cola on offer in the nearby shop if we bothered to queue.

Despite the general weariness amongst our party, a certain jollity prevailed, with our resident comedians settling into some gentle banter with Des, aka Mr Moustache. Nick the Giggler had everyone in fits of laughter, regaling us with the tale of his much-anticipated sleepover in the girls' tent last night, only to be confronted by loud snores long before lights out.

'Civilisation at last,' I gasped as we pulled onto the hotel forecourt.

'Oh, Trod, I have never been so pleased to see a hotel in all my life. It's like an oasis.'

The drivers worked quickly and, before long, we were all dragging dirty packs into our rooms, Sarah rummaging for suitable clothing for a *hammam* visit.

'Are you sure it's not for you, Dawne? Just think, an all-over soaping and a muscle-relaxing backrub. What a way to get rid of all the dirt.'

'You go on. I'll give it a miss.' The perfect end to our trip was my idea of hell. Anyone rubbing my back was likely to receive a swift thump from me.

'Just before you join everyone, take a picture of me, would you? I'd like the "after" photo.'

Weary trekker One, back at the hotel.

'Oh, me too. We look pretty ragged compared to just a few days ago. Your clothes are loose on you.' With that, I stepped out of my filthy trekking trousers without undoing the zip. The weight had fallen off me.

As far as I was concerned, I had the best treat, taking the longest and most welcome shower of my life in the bathroom tiled in the traditional Arabic blue and yellow motifs.

The hotel wasn't comfortable in the western style but perfectly adequate for our needs on our Charity Challenge budget. It wouldn't have felt right to splash the cash on somewhere luxurious when we were all trying to raise funds for our various causes. As far as I was concerned, hot water, clean towels and a flushing toilet and, for later on, cool and clean sheets on a soft bed would suffice.

Weary trekker Two.

Even before I could take that longed-for shower, there was a loud knock on the door. Rushing to open it, my heart was flying in the knowledge that Bernie had arrived to greet me. It was worth it, for the biggest hug a girl could ever want.

He had driven over the mountains from Marrakech that day and was full of tales of his journey, allowing me space to drink in his presence.

'I'm so proud of you.' His first words made me weepy yet again.

'I'm very stinky, you know,' I pointed out to cover the emotions spilling over.

'Tell you what, I need to eat, and you want your shower and dinner with your friends. So, I'll see you later.' Eager not to distract me from my last hours with the group, he took himself off, leaving me to luxuriate in abundant hot water.

'You weren't long, Sarah. How was the *hammam*?'

'Oh, quite one of the best experiences of my life. They did pummel you a bit though, so it was just as well you didn't join us. Is Bernie here yet?'

'Oh, yes, the warmest cuddle of my life. He's leaving us to it for the time being, as I want to be here with you. I can catch up with him soon enough.'

'OK. So, one or two people want to hit the nearby *souks* for some gifts to take home. I fancy a wander around too. Are you going to come?'

'Yes, I will. I'll be ready in five minutes. Are we meeting in the lobby?'

'Don't forget your purse. We might actually need some money for this part of our trip.'

Souks are markets found in all Moroccan towns, usually full of stalls and small shops, all jumbled together along winding alleyways and thronged with shoppers. We had to be careful not to get lost.

Colourful displays of stained-glass lamps spilled out onto the pavements, along with small shops full of leather slippers with turned-up toes, silver jewellery and much more besides. We were spoiled for choice.

'Come on, Sarah, let's look in here,' I said, pulling her into yet another warren of shops, one leading into another, shoes and leather jackets in unsteady heaps all around us.

'Don't you think it smells a bit funny here?'

'It's all a bit stinky if you ask me,' I replied. 'Moroccan drains aren't up to much, are they? There's

196

also a line of donkeys outside, tied to the railing. I think they're for sale. They're pretty smelly too.'

'Oh, I'm just trying to ignore all that. It's nothing like as bad as our toilet pit, is it? I mean the clothes and leather goods.'

'Oh, that,' I replied, laughing. 'This is where those horrible old camels end up, you know.'

'No, really?' My mate was horrified, immediately putting down the jacket she had been looking at.

'They smell dreadful when they get wet,' I continued, giggling at the expression of distaste on her face.

'Let's get out of here. I think I've seen enough, and I'm sure it's nearly time for dinner.'

As we wended our way back towards the hotel, the traditionally dressed shopkeepers were cheeky, daring us to come inside.

'Looky, looky, you looky. Good prices. Come in, we have mint tea for you.' They were disappointed as we declined to haggle for any more bargains.

It is quite normal in Morocco to overhear shouts and arguments as you pass by the shops. Thinking there was something dreadful going on, we poked our heads around a couple of doorways, only to find some lively haggling taking place. I'm hopeless at it, but some of our gang had a lot of fun bargaining down prices.

The *souk* visit had been interesting, but the markets had been cleaned up to appeal to visitors. I have been into the northern Moroccan towns before where there were dirty, noisy areas full of animals, cheek by jowl with butcher's shops with bloody hunks of meat hanging outside. It had been enough to turn me vegetarian. There would be clothing next to homeware and hardware stalls, even shoe repair shacks and all manner of other small businesses. This was tame in comparison.

I'm sure we were a sight for sore eyes. Most of us were clean but still dishevelled, wearing whatever crumpled clothing we still had that wasn't filthy.

We didn't have long to mooch around. Despite the lack of time, we all managed to pick up some bits and pieces to take home as souvenirs.

Of course, much of it was easily available in southern Spain, so I concentrated on helping Sarah find her treasures. Soaking up the atmosphere, which was all very light-hearted, the local traders were obviously used to visitors who wouldn't be bullied by their sales tactics. Although, I sensed that things could change quickly from friendly to sinister and threatening in just a few short moments.

Back from our shopping expedition, we hurriedly changed into our least dirty gear and, amazingly, we thought we had scrubbed up quite well, although we hadn't brought makeup with us as we had thought it would be surplus to requirements. Some of the girls looked positively glamorous.

Heading into the bar, cold beer sang its siren song to us.

'Cheers, Trod.' Hugging one another yet again, I think we would both agree that the first icy cold beer was probably the best one of our lives. Well-deserved too. As it slipped down, I felt the first glimmerings of relaxation creeping into my weary body.

Our group had a reserved table for dinner, and we took up a large part of the restaurant. Enormous terracotta dishes were laid out on the buffet table for us to help ourselves, although few of us ate very much. Most of our party had tummy troubles, and we were too tired to be truly hungry. I think we were saving our energy for the partying to come.

Congregating in the bar later, you could see the tension drain away. Beaming smiles, aches and pains forgotten, we were intent on celebrating our achievements.

Of course, a few words had to be said. Des spoke for us trekkers, thanking Nia and Angela for their efforts to keep us motivated and, above all, safe on our adventure.

The climax of the evening was the handing out of the Charity Challenge Oscars. Nia and Angela had been busy noting all our quirks and foibles, and we all came in for some gentle teasing. Medals were handed out to each of us with some film-related comment. Sarah and I were Thelma and Louise, from the film of the same name. As my friend had never seen it, I vowed to post her a copy as soon as we got home.

In the bar, tired but happy.

Our evening soon degenerated into karaoke and group dancing, faces shining in the soft lighting as we all wound down quite quickly, knowing it was an early start in the morning.

Bernie joined us for a while, listening to the general gossip and hilarity, but by midnight it was time to head off to our beds.

I said a weary goodnight and left him at his bedroom door as I had promised to spend every moment of the trek with Sarah. She had a wake-up call in just four short hours, along with all those going back to the UK, and I had resolved to get up and wave them off. My longed-for cuddle from Bernie would have to wait.

'Beep, beep.' The alarm cut rudely into our light sleep. There hadn't been much time to switch off, as we hadn't been able to resist a chat about the events of our final evening.

'Blimey, Dawne, I don't feel as if we had time to sleep at all.'

'I seem to remember you doing some pretty heavy breathing, so you must have slept a little. You'll spend the next week catching up at home.'

'Why don't you stay in bed?'

'No, I'm well and truly awake now, and I want to say a proper goodbye to you all.'

'OK. Leave my bags, I can manage. You can hold the doors open if you like.'

'The jeeps are here, so pick up your packs,' Angela called, once again busy organising everyone. It all happened so quickly that it was a minute or two before an abrupt sense of loss flooded through me. I had waved them goodbye with hugs all round, and they were gone, leaving me to wander back to my room alone, wondering when Bernie would knock on my door and our own adventure begin. I just wanted to sleep for a week.

EPILOGUE
What Happened Next

With the benefit of hindsight, I can see what a marvellous experience this was. It turned out to be one of the toughest challenges of my life, and I only wish that I could have enjoyed the actual trek itself more.

Bernie and I spent a few days in Morocco, and it was just as well we whizzed around by car as I was exhausted and in considerable pain, little better than a washed-out wraith.

Trying to cut down on painkillers didn't help. I needed them more than ever now as my back complained about the punishment I had put it through over the past week. I couldn't wait to get home and rest with gentle exercise to keep things from stiffening up. Gradual improvement took three months.

I thought at the time that this was the adventure of a lifetime, and that it was just a one-off experience. However, since then, things have rolled along, and my love of fundraising remains.

Five months after my return, we managed to organise the postponed "Not So Strictly!" dance competition. With only two weeks of hectic training, I was never going to be an expert dancer, but it turned out to be lots of fun, and I like to think I acquitted myself quite well.

However, nerves certainly got the better of me. Unless you have done it yourself, you have no idea how daunting it can be to put yourself in the spotlight like that, and I couldn't have done it without support from Ian and Rebecca at Pickles Dance School.

My fellow competitors all entered into the spirit of the event and our raffle raised over four hundred euros for the charity. I was very happy with that.

Fundraising continues and I think it will be a lifelong commitment for me to support Thrombosis UK in spreading the word about blood clots.

A recent forty-eight-kilometre walk over one hot, sultry August night into the mountains of Mallorca seemed like a good idea at the time....but that could be another story.

****

CONTACT THE AUTHOR

Thank you for reading this book, and I hope you enjoyed it. Reviews are helpful to authors, so I would be grateful if you would take the time to leave one on Amazon. Just a few words, or a lot, it doesn't matter.

Come and join my Facebook author page which can be found at
www.facebook.com/TrekkerGirl2012/

I would also be delighted if you join me on Twitter at @DawneArcher19

I am happy to answer any questions you may have, so please do get in touch at
trekkergirl@outlook.com

If you enjoy reading memoirs, I recommend you join the Facebook group We Love Memoirs where you can chat with other readers and authors as well as me. You can find us here
www.facebook.com/groups/welovememoirs

In my opinion, this is the best group on Facebook with interesting content, supportive members and full of other memoir recommendations.

Printed in Great Britain
by Amazon